STARTUP
FEVER

STARTUP FEVER

How Crowdfunding Will Rebuild the American Dream

AUSTIN MUHS

Why You Must Read This Book…

Being an entrepreneur I have always understood the unknown perils of striking out on your own into uncharted waters, in order to test your theological business acumen against the hand of fate. If I were to say that this is a quest without danger, I would obviously be lying to you and not doing you much good in the process. I have personally started 7 small businesses, or startups depending on how you want to classify the term. I started all of these businesses with little to no upfront money, and eventually turned a profit with all seven of them. This is a process also known as bootstrapping within the Startup community; as you are stuck digging into your own pockets to finance your personal vocational dreams.

During my time bootstrapping, I have seen my fair share of the good, the bad, and the ugly; and I wanted to set out on a quest for the rectification of what I feel like are the unpleasant things within the business community––as well as clear up any misconceptions that people may have received about what it means to have a meaningful career, or vocation, within this country. I wanted people to know what it feels like to go through hell and back starting up businesses, while sparing them the purchase of flame-retardant attire. Since I have learned to stop, drop, and roll with the best of them, I know that you will find value in what this text has to offer.

Being that the odds in this country seem to be ever mounting against small businesses, I feel it is absolutely crucial that these new ideologies emerging around crowdfunding be adopted in an expedient, open-minded, and morally virtuous fashion. As of yet, we have seen little to emerge from the crowdfunding vehicle other than a few new techno gadgets, charitable foundations, and some of the latest indie artist fare. While I know in my heart and soul that so much more is in store for this economic sea change, as it represents us taking our power back from the larger institutions of society-which have held us prisoner with our own capital. Taking our hard-earned money for granted and leaving us with a pale shadow of what the American Dream might have once meant to the great men and women who died in their pursuit of vocational and ideological freedom; men and women who fought to eliminate the taxes, and the entrepreneurial oppression that had existed in times past.

To me, crowdfunding represents the rebirth of a true America; and an America of which we can truly be proud to call home. It is an absolute means to reestablishing a sense of community, while still integrating the new wave of technological innovation that Americans so unanimously love, in a healthier way. Should we not utilize this grand opportunity in human history to change our collective fate and reemerge as the masters of our own destiny? We will have lost one of the key theological battles in human history in my opinion if we do nothing.

One of my favorite quotes of all time comes from Abraham Lincoln, who said: "If you gave me 8 hours to chop down a tree, I would spend six hours sharpening the ax." Which is exactly where I see this book coming in handy. Coming from a background in which I have been forced to chop down many an obstacle, I have also been chased around by an ax as well (metaphorically). So, I can tell you firsthand about how this new wave of innovations and technologies will make it much less risky than in times past to pursue your vocational destiny.

Contents

Introduction

So, I stand here before you at the peak of modern civilization; a time just as regressive as any other in our modern psychological history—an age where modern man calls upon science to solve all of his existential quandaries. Generally speaking, Western society has said "to hell" with finding the answers to life through self-assertion—or through the quest of developing an individualistic will. Society has instead, by and large, decided that they will leave their peers to tackle this process; or conversely, that they are just not up to the task of building themselves a soul. Although most people will readily ignore this calling toward humanistic self-creation, I feel that meaningful internal dialogue about the purpose of your existence is the only thing capable of leading us toward a passionate and profitable vocation.

In my time in the entrepreneurial community, I have come to realize that any business with true longevity is more about serving the customer than serving the self. I have tried to create ventures that mostly served to enrich my bank account. Such as my foray into online Facebook promotion with Pay For Friends or promotion for restaurants through Catering Promoters; but, ultimately, fate led me away from these ventures—ventures that did not serve my personal development goals in the long term. In essence, they brought nothing truly idiosyncratic to the table; and, therefore, were ultimately unsustainable. Even if they did serve to teach me specific skills I would need later on, they were unable to hold my interest and my spiritual need for a passionate vocation. As even with a good paycheck, without a challenge or enrichment: what was the point?

While most worldly people thoroughly celebrate collective self-avoidance, what they fail to understand is that this avoidance simultaneously condemns them to a purposeless career. Why do many people dislike their job? That's because they have listened to advice from other similarly dissatisfied career malcontents. Preferring to take the standard career road, instead of opening up to the possibilities of what could be. These thoughtless types of careers only serve to build more psychological barriers; barriers that the rest of society must eventually tear down. This is why meaningful vocational change for our kind is so difficult; half of us are locked away in corporate dungeons of all shape and size, effectively being protected from any emotional involvement with nature or the rest of the world.

In actuality, in the beginning of my startup life, I was no different. I was as self-avoidant as anyone, dreaming of illusory monetary dominance with no true merit or skill set to back up my aims—hoping that money would somehow help me to find my place and meaning in the cosmos. Although I knew deep down that one day I would find meaning for myself in the business world, I just had no clue that it would involve such an unconventional career track. Instead of building up my skill set, I was busy shielding myself from the hardships and true accountability necessary in the entrepreneurial world. Accountability meant I would have to take a good hard look at my less desirable traits and penchant for self-sabotage. I was following in the footsteps of my parents who were both in sales despite the fact that they were both perpetually stressed out. I was adorning the suit of the common worker bee, hoping to find my success through the traditional salesman route.

While times may change many methods remain the same. In my estimation business really is a modern type of warfare and should be viewed as such. Anyone who has ever been sitting on the other end of a nasty attorney knows this to be the case. We are in a battle, a battle for our collective psychic freedom. In an age where capturing people in the traditional "prisoner" sense has become too impractical and cumbersome, collective thought has become the modern-day prison. We are in a fight for our lives and it's important that we treat every day as the most important opportunity that we have ever been given. Despite all the tyrannical bureaucracy coming out of the U.S. business world, it still represents our best chance for existential freedom in the modern times.

Again, all we need to do is look out the nearest window to find evidence for a plethora of unhappy vocational quitters. Besides just being a slave to the clock, the un-expounded, theologically bereft, modern man remains a slave to himself. We have become the oppressors of our own dreams, held captive by our inner psychological dictators. Does your career need to have meaning if your sole objective is to acquire more money? Especially when you're only using the money to run further away from yourself, purchasing distractions of every shape and size. Humanity is full of lost souls stuck on repeat: partying day and night, numbing themselves to sleep at night. They are always in need of more funding to quench the thirst of the insatiable shadow side within. It's like a vocational *Groundhog Day* scenario, where conformity is the rule, not the exception, and a lack of fulfillment is the unfortunate result. I can assure you that as a nation the only path back to the good life, lies in confronting ourselves. Obviously, not everyone you meet will be up to the task; but for those who are willing and able, it represents something that must be done before any meaningful stability can be maintained. So, it's time to sit down and figure out this whole concept of the new American Dream; because the old one has died and no one has been notified of the funeral.

The process of willful self-ignorance being perpetuated by the masses is condemning us to a spiritual holding pattern, further delaying our true evolution as a species. "But wait," you might be asking, "isn't this supposed to be a business book?" Well, yes and no; because I believe the true roots to the problem of vocational fulfillment lie in this search for a regimented carefree utopia. In order to find legitimate and lasting answers to our deepest questions, we must dare to look outside of the feedback loop happening outside our window. Instead of internal challenges, many people have come to the conclusion that science will handle all of these difficult life questions— creating a culture of technology without individuality.

What about the true meaning of our existence? We can depend on science to show us the way to true fulfillment, right? Wrong. Despite man's best attempts, science has not, will not, and will never be able to answer these complex questions—let alone begin to heal the traumatized, emotionally fragmented, technologically perverse state we find ourselves in. No number of Albert Einsteins or techno gadgets will ever be able to make you feel comfortable living in your own head. Individualistic self-acclimatization is a lifelong task we must take on by ourselves and pursue for our own good. Granted, there will be an ample amount of teaching and guidance for us along the way; the fate of our own psychological development, and therefore the development of our external vocational progress, is up to us.

This new type of dogmatic rhetoric, of searching for spirituality through a microscope, has made it difficult for us to visualize a new template for economic development in the outside word. The disconnection of our spiritual and moral development from our inherent vocational money-making abilities has left many people working in a corporate wasteland of meaningless monotony. An institutionalized *Groundhog Day* meets *Office Space* pan-inter-dimensional-succubus scenario that can leave even the bravest of souls feeling flustered. But don't lose hope yet! The destruction of this seemingly impenetrable corporate fortress is easier than it looks. In fact, it's already happening on many levels; and it promises to be a self-destruction for the ages, as the tools needed to rebuild a saner and emotionally and spiritually connected future are already here.

The crowdfunding model represents a vast arsenal of psychological weaponry to get a healthy economy back and running—while staving off any would-be economic big bad wolves that come to blow our house down. This is possible because crowdfunding represents a decentralized model of working together with your fellow man in smaller groups; groups small enough to maintain accountability, transparency, and perhaps even sanity.

To address the problems astutely, we must understand that the lack of overall moral development within our species is no accident. Modern social planners have worked tirelessly to breed us into the perfect consumer clones. This high-tech psychological assault on our spiritual consciousness seems to get more egregious by the day—a process of which most people are unaware. The gluttony of the spiritually perverse media invading our unwitting psyches represents a form of poison to our souls. The results of these programming efforts can be witnessed in the breaking apart of the family unit and the gross neglect of any tasks that involve true individuality.

If you want to find out the effects of these programming mechanisms on the younger generations, you can just go and talk to the ever-growing group of local divorcees in your town. I'm sure you can find a few of these characters at the nearest dive bar. They will tell you how a halfhearted, half-sober effort at maintaining a family unit plays out. I know the destruction that follows in the wake of pretentious and hedonistic family units, as I have seen these types of families by the hundreds all over America. I have lived a few places and traveled to a few more; and I can assure you that in America, the broken home is the new normal.

Again, I'm not up on a high horse here, as I hail from a broken home myself. I grew up watching the middle class crumble beneath my feet—heralded by false religious dogmas and dishonest consumerist utopias. So, I should know. The pursuit of pleasure for its own sake is a black hole which makes orphans of your emotions and beggars of your children; this is the plague from which we suffer. How long must we let our insatiable desires dictate our entire culture? At this rate, we will soon be buying our marriage licenses from a vending machine and hiring robots to raise our children. Now, perhaps, society should look at other possibilities that don't involve marriage. All I know is that the new wave of subconscious media programming has all but destroyed the traditional family unit.

Instead of learning more about ourselves, we have become part of a trite collective of entertainment addicts––a society that will consume nearly any form of entertainment, no matter how toxic, in an attempt to avoid self-analysis. I am convinced that if advanced aliens were to land on our planet today, they would think we were a bunch of trained chimps. Many of us spew the same tired phrases and hang at the same watering holes while exuding the same type of existential boredom; mindlessly staring at flickering boxes hung all over town for hours on end— relating to each other only in proximity to what entertainment activities we have recently enjoyed.

As strange as it may seem, some of the only individuality left in our society stems from the business world—perhaps even more so than the arts, in their current state of spiritual dilapidation. Young minds across the country are working double-time trying to figure out how to make a living in a job market that seems to only provide for those with Ivy League credentials. If you find yourself in the pool of people who did not graduate from a prestigious university, or with a rock star skill set in some form of professional sport, you might have to try your hand at entrepreneurship if you are aiming for long-term vocational fulfillment.

Anyone who has had to work in a lower-level job should be able to realize that no company has your utmost happiness in mind when they hire you. For most large corporations, you are just a digit on a screen, a replaceable trainee. Now in one-sense that's fine as it was your decision to take the job, but on another level, it points us toward the deeper issues confronting our economic purpose. I don't have to tell anyone that any focus on personal growth is almost non-existent in the low level jobs across America. These are the same corporations who wonder why they can't cultivate a corporate culture of innovation to keep up with the competition; if they had only had the foresight to nurture talent from within.

Oddly, the new *Lego Movie* points out this whole theme of self-creation brilliantly, where all of the coolest Lego people in the kingdom are what they call the "Master Builders"—a term that comes from the occult science of numerology. These "Master Builders" represent the coolest and happiest people in the Lego kingdom, as they are the ones who actively go out and create their own realities. They are also the ones responsible for fighting against "Mr. Corporate," who seeks to create perpetual conformity within the other Lego citizens. The movie is a clear illustration for children that the most interesting people go out and create their own world; or, more eloquently, they allow the world that they want to live in to build itself.

A meaningful vocation requires more than just a good paycheck or a fancy office. It requires a true passion for existence; many times, that passion for existence extends beyond you, to helping others out in the world. For the self-motivated individual, entrepreneurship can present one of the only options to achieve true personal fulfillment.

I wanted to write a book that helps people seize the opportunity to build a business during any adverse circumstance life might bring. While also showing them the purpose behind the process so that we can start to understand that a different type of American Dream might make more sense—a dream where fiscal predictability is replaced by individualistic achievement and moral development. I can say from experience that some of the happiest times in my life occurred when I had almost nothing. During those times, I started to understand how my superficial needs were standing in the way of my own evolution. I wanted more "stuff," but I didn't know why. It just seemed like the right thing to do. Children are a prime example of the less-is-more philosophy. Children naturally exude the purest and most serene sense of joy that you will ever be blessed to encounter—possessions being the least of their concerns. They are happy and amused sitting and playing with a set of keys—or in some imaginary world of their own creation. What they are really displaying is a natural inclination to live in their own internal universe. This internal universe is a place many adults have totally forgotten about—cutting themselves off from the true source of their creativity. It doesn't take a genius to realize that children are much closer to pure creativity than many of their adult counterparts. As such, children make invaluable teachers in many regards. What does a child really need to be happy: love, sanity, communication, food, shelter, water? These are needs that are pretty easily met on a base level.

START-UP FEVER

Perhaps this is all any of us truly need, as I don't think that a child is really worrying about whether daddy will become some kind of corporate mogul or if mommy will be a bestselling author. It is also pretty obvious that when we die, we don't get to take much with us. We do, on the other hand, get to leave behind a little thing called a legacy. And if you are lucky, that legacy will point humanity toward a brighter future. A future where others will utter your name in reference to all the things in this world that are holy and sane—a life which was dedicated to something beyond personal gratification. That type of life is a life truly worth living.

Whether we realize it or not, a new epoch of synergistic business development is upon us—an economic shift that is bound to bring us back into contact with the natural rhythms of the world; and if we're lucky, allow us to reclaim the vocational birthrights of our species. Within that quest, we will be required to forge a long-term commitment to building our soul, sometimes from the ground up. We must construct souls that are not vulnerable to the most astute and psychologically nefarious corporate technocratic control system that the world has ever seen. A media-based system carefully crafted by the worldwide power structures to lead us away from true spiritual freedom. This is a system that ultimately wants to lead us away from ourselves, while chaining us to superficial pursuits. The powers that be have never had a vested interest in helping people to find fiscal empowerment. We must realize there is nothing wrong with money, only with its immorally apportionment in the outside world.

By letting go of the world that has been handed to us, we can fully embrace a world which we have yet to create. On the upside, much can be salvaged out of the old system. The time is upon us; and if we are aware of it, we can be at the forefront of an economic renaissance the likes of which the world has ever seen. As entrepreneurs build an identity or brand for their business, they are also helping to externalize a part of our internal life which they would like to share with the world.

I write in the sincere hope that people get excited, energized, and motivated about cultivating something meaningful within their lives. When we are in tune with our vocational purpose, we project that harmoniously passionate state out into the economic community at-large. Many people within the realm of financial forecasting are busy spewing out doom and gloom due to the dismal state of world economics; when in actuality, there has probably never been a better time to start a new business—as a unique opportunity for vocational fulfillment lies in crowdfunding, the likes of which has never been seen before. Startups can achieve massive success in week instead of years, as they are able to actively create a solid base of clientele while raising funds for their dream at the same time.

Looking at the boom-and-bust cycles of other unstable economies, you begin to realize that this instability actually drives ingenuity. During this change in global-financing practices, growth is possible in areas where it was previously unapproachable—as change truly is the only constant in the universe and nothing lasts forever. Destruction breeds creation, as the old adage goes. This is an important phrase for all of us to remember, as the constancy of life in this dimension has a finite quality to it. Think about it? I'm sure there were larger business concerns outside of the monarchy during the renaissance, yet none readily come to mind. Except perhaps the East Indian Trading Company out of England. So, we must realize that businesses in the tangible goods sense usually don't last forever.

Through history, we can also infer that economies naturally move toward ensconced monopolies. Knowing this, we can maintain an objective and dispassionate viewpoint about the situation at hand. Economic oppression has happened before on the earth and it will happen again; yet, these types of systems all inevitably crumble. The greed and gluttony produced by malevolent monopolies eventually leads to an economic decomposition from the inside out. This is the situation we find ourselves in today.

We need not feel forlorn. Disruptive businesses and technologies will always exist. These are the natural protection mechanisms built within nature to restore balance no matter how insane society might become. There is no such thing as a perfect monopoly or total control for that matter. These concepts are merely illusions rooted in the darker parts of the human mind. There will always be brilliant souls within the consciousness of humanity that come along to upset the apple cart. The genius renegades such as Nikola Tesla, Johannes Gutenberg, Lu Donbing, and Buckminster Fuller will always exist; thereby, giving the established business oligarchs a run for their money. This process is described in the *Tao Te Ching*—also known as the book of changes.

> "In the world nothing is more fragile than water, and yet of all the agencies that attack hard substances, nothing can surpass it. Of all things, there is nothing that can take the place of Tao. By it the weak are conquerors of the strong, the pliable

are conquerors of the rigid. In the world everyone knows this, but none practice it. Therefore the wise man declares: he who is guilty of the country's sin may be the priest at the altar. He, who is to blame for the country's misfortunes, is often the Empire's Sovereign. True words are often paradoxical."
Translated by <u>Dwight Goddard</u>, 1919, Chapter 78, *Tao Te Ching*

For a long while I have wanted to share my vision of how start-ups of the future will take on a much different shape than the current models we see in place today. As my friend Lane pointed out (a cutting-edge crowd-funder himself), crowdfunding isn't changing the world; it's already changed it. Businesses are now in the process of trying to catch up. Although there have been subtle allusions to what changes will actually come about within the next few decades, much of it will actually depend on the twenty-somethings of today. The younger age groups, such as Gen-Y and "the millennials" as they are called, are under more pressure than ever to create purpose within a consumer-driven world. Even though on the surface these younger folks may seem a bit entitled and lost, from my experience many of them are capable of great feats when fate dictates the unveiling of their true nature. When adversity strikes, it forces people to look inward for their answers. This so-called negative "adversity" can allow for a cathartic psychological energy to take hold, ultimately leading to a profound reformation. A revolution of vocational purpose can help even the most desperate souls to once again find their place in life. By providing emotional and spiritual context into these internal changes, we might be able to

13

profit from our own economic uncertainty. Expecting things to stay the same forever is an illusion of the human ego; and the less dependent we are upon a fixed state of affairs in the business world, the better off we will be.

Although our species faces many problems of enigmatic enormity, I only propose to deal with a few of them. Namely, trying to figure out how the human species can create greater meaning for themselves and how we can develop a sustainable model to grow small businesses in the future—while also integrating emotional, spiritual, and psychological development into the mix as well.

Even with access to seemingly unlimited amounts of information, why do the basic questions of human existence remain as perplexing as ever? Why can't we discover our true meaning once and for all? It seems that if we have shown up on this strange place called Earth, there has to be a reason. And if we are going to spend most of the productive span of our lifetime utilizing our talents toward building goods and services out in society, then our vocational purpose probably has a good bit to do with the reason we are alive. As fate would have it, finding this vocational purpose can be quite a chore. It remains a chore because you're the only one who can solve these deeper questions about your life—not your leaders, not society, not the latest movie star. Just you!

Even though we are stuck in a land of almost total uncertainty, we are still blessed with the ability to conjure solutions to any problems we may face—no matter how complex the problem might be. This is because at the same instant that a problem is born within our minds, the answer has also simultaneously arisen; only, it is up to us to discover it! I like to look at life like a giant Rubik's cube:

life is not a "problem" to be solved, but rather an exercise in putting ourselves back into proper alignment within. All the while trying to let go of the extraneous blocks that other people have glued on to us—blocks that they would like us to believe are our own. We still struggle to find our true form and perhaps we do not understand our ultimate form until the day of our death; all I can say is that it is not what society tells us it is. Our true self is something we must discover all on our lonesome. It's a simple formula. In the words of Abraham Lincoln: "When I do good, I feel good; when I do bad, I feel bad: that is my religion."

Even though our quest for selfhood has become more obscured in many regards, the path toward vocational purpose has never been more direct. We live in an age that has unequivocally given us the tools to meet our employment aims. Personal destiny aside, fulfilling employment is a major key to long-term purpose and happiness; and fiscal stability is a key to spiritual progress as well, despite what many would have you believe. The "masterminds" behind the current economic system would love us to equate money with enlightenment; hence, the massive use of symbolism involved with money. They wouldn't put all of those fancy unintelligible symbols on the paper bills if they didn't want the old greenback to resonate with our subconscious need for meaning in life. Even though money doesn't represent spiritual attainment; in and of itself, it still can be a powerful tool toward achieving needed reforms in the outside world. Sometimes, we need to reform business systems; other times, we need to reform our housing to achieve another level of growth. Whatever you need money for: I aim to show that, ultimately, as long as true growth for humanity at-large is the motive, money can help us achieve anything we want. It is only when money sits still and stagnates that it becomes a tool for evil deeds. As long as it is flowing vigorously, a healthy relationship with money can always be maintained. Crowdfunding represents an important tool for helping humanity develop a healthier relationship to both vocationalism and wealth.

It is my earnest hope that this book illuminates the forces that are driving the new wave of crowdfunding infrastructure and to show how they might best be utilized going forward. This truly is a spiritual phenomenon that if used correctly is capable of changing the economic landscape forever. Crowdfunding is amazing as it opens up entrepreneurship to people of any background. No longer do you need an MBA or anything of the sort to acquire small business financing. Anyone who has access to the Internet and a video capable smartphone could theoretically take part in helping to rebuild the world economics. There really is no good excuse not to take part in this virtual boomtown.

Ch. 0

Choosing your Funding

Much of entrepreneurial life involves allowing for enough internal latitude to make some mistakes. Oftentimes, people get hung up on waiting for the perfect scenario for a startup. If this is you, I have a little news for you: nothing is perfect and startups rarely get traction due to some Hail Mary angel investor. Angel investors are those entrepreneurially minded investors who are willing to take high risks on smaller startups to reap potentially massive gains by backing the right horse. Generally, these people hedge their bets and place money with a basket of different startups—instead of expecting eggs from a lone golden goose. If you're waiting on money like that with no proven track record or high level MBA background, then you might as well keep buying lotto tickets and schmoozing it up at the local bingo night because it's not looking good for you. Having had many a millionaire investor promise me this and that, I realized that most of it was hot air. Unless it's family money, or some serious windfall scenario, even seasoned angels are hesitant to pull the trigger until things are airtight. Not to mention the fact that many of them don't deal directly with investments, preferring to have their investment manager handle it for them. Even if you do find the money through some miracle person, there's no guarantee they are a quality investor. Will that miracle cash-flow also come with unethical motives—or other strings attached that will end up sinking your business long term? These scenarios are all possible and they happen all the time. In my experience, trusting your gut and not being afraid to take risks will get you much further.

Although crowdfunding will allow unparalleled access to new funding, investor discernment is always advised. If you were looking to get funding through a few major players instead of starting a general crowd fund, I would always recommend leaning toward finding investors who are well versed in the field that your company is in. You want someone investing who understands your model and who understands where you're trying to go. Silent investors are fine and dandy; but if you get into a pinch looking for that next level of expansion, then you're going to want someone with whom to talk to about it. It's always good to go for the less-emotional type of investors as well. You want people who won't hassle you as long as you are delivering your end of the work on time. Emotional types usually want to check in and second guess what you're doing if they have nothing better to do. These are the paid friend kind of guys and they can become a hassle when you're trying to juggle projects.

There is also the other type of controlling investors who might not be comfortable if you're not under their thumb. At the end of the day, psychological due diligence is a must. I personally consult with reputable astrologers, or other psychological experts, to double check major decisions from a subconscious perspective. Although I am well versed in many of these methodologies as well, it never hurts to get a second opinion. The more you are involved in business, the more you will be able to spot other people's insecurities and personality types right off the bat; thereby, avoiding much hassle and heartache if things don't go right. Bottom line: you must also do your psychological due diligence, as the wrong investor can really cause serious upheaval in your life.

I have heard many a horror story about investors gone wrong. Some investors want to micromanage to the nth degree, causing undue pressure upon the business. One guy I know recently took money from a lifelong accountant, who wanted mountains of inventory and personal reports to be filed every day. Literally, this investor wanted 12-15 pages of paperwork daily, in a very high-stress small business, where the owner simply wouldn't have time for it. Long story short, the business owner took a bath on the newly purchased equipment and lost 80-100 hours of productivity due to the drama that ensued.

Another story involved a large-scale investor who liked to get drunk and brag at parties, effectively spilling trade secrets and tarnishing the company reputation at key industry-related functions where discretion would normally be advised. A scenario that eventually scared off other investors and forced the company to scale down, when they could have been just ramping up.

Heck, some people invest just so they can get some kicks out of throwing their weight around—or to brag at their hip watering hole. This "ego investment" can get really ugly if you're not careful, so it pays to do your homework. Hell, run a background check if you have to.

Look for the litigious types who might want to draw you in with an unscrupulous contract they know you can't decipher—only to later take over via legal means. There are also other types of authoritarian personalities that would serve to destroy you out of jealousy, or envy, of your virtuous nature. Never be afraid to walk away if something smells fishy. Investors who rush in to give you cash without doing their due diligence can have ulterior motives, especially when large sums are concerned.

10 Steps Ahead

As the traditional economic financing engines (i.e. the mega banks) grind small business financing to a halt—as well as tighten up on personal lines of credit—entrepreneurs must start to create alternative solutions to the issue of financing. Inevitably, the politicians will come along and syphon off this new wellspring of American innovation, so adaptability must remain a big part of the plan. Not only will the government want a cut, but also these very same politicos will always deny any fault in an economic downturn. Heaven forbid anyone point the finger at the bloated bureaucracies and extortionist policies that are dismantling the traditional small business financing engines. Long story short, you can't depend on long-term funding from the government because, theologically speaking, governments are wealth-management mechanisms, not wealth-creation mechanisms. Anyone who thinks otherwise is sadly mistaken.

Even if they tried to create wealth, it's just not in their nature; any more than it's in my nature to go and work a mindless desk job somewhere. No matter how hard I try, even my best efforts at enslaving myself at a desk would only go so far. I feel the government's best efforts would also be met with just such lackluster results. The best a government can do is to prevent criminality in industry and keep people safe from work-related hazards in the process. America will soon start to understand that financing is something we would do better to handle on our own local level. I wouldn't depend on the government for anything but red tape in the near future—except perhaps a swift kick to the teeth or higher taxes, which are always in high supply. The best we can hope for going forward is a more decentralized economic engine and perhaps competing currencies; but until that happens, we need to be pragmatic and prepared for economic self-sufficiency. One of the veteran mentors on economic self-sufficiency was the late Ayn Rand, a must read for any aspiring entrepreneurial mind. Her seminal work is, of course, "Atlas Shrugged."

> "If you ask me to name the proudest distinction of Americans, I would choose—because it contains all the others—the fact that they were the people who created the phrase 'to make money.' No other language or nation had ever used these words before; men had always thought of wealth as a static quantity—to be seized, begged, inherited, shared, looted or obtained as a favor. Americans were the first to understand that wealth has to be created."
> —Ayn Rand, "Atlas Shrugged"

START-UP FEVER

Restructuring the economy into a more sustainable format is something that we must take on ourselves. That's right, I said it, we need to let go of the mommy-and-daddy-handholding operation and go out there and start flying solo. There's no need to "what if" a project to death. In reality, there are a thousand reasons why you could go out of business, losing your shirt in the process; but by the same token, there are a thousand-and-one ways to build a healthy happy and fiscally successful business within your community. As long as you build something that actually helps people and does good work, you should be able to keep it afloat. From my experience, the universe seems to always take care of morally virtuous people.

Build a professional team you can trust and try to work with your local economy, where applicable. If the world is against the small guy, so be it; take heart in the challenge! Embrace the fact that sometimes the hardest path is the most rewarding. The oppressive forces within the universe give you a chance to uncover the diamonds of the soul, so to hell with the naysayers! Big business has always seen small business as a threat to their market share, but that doesn't mean you shouldn't put up a fight. In summary, within our newly emerging economic system becoming profitable quickly is more important than ever, as long-term financing will soon dry up for those who are not cash solvent, or involved with a corporate interest large enough to warrant consideration from the big banks.

The formation of the micro-funding and crowdfunding mechanisms, as well as the crypto-currency phenomenon, are all important steps toward restoring hope for small business in the future. As far as currency solutions go, cash will always be king—and barter can only take us so far. Gold and silver have become a bit impractical for everyday use in today's internet-based marketplace; so, something else must inevitably emerge. Crypto-currencies, unfortunately, will never be able to bear the full weight of the economic load in my estimation due not only to possible manipulation, but also mostly due to the fact that the transactions are only as safe as the websites they are on. The web will never be 100% secure, as no internet security system is foolproof.

What happens when eBay decides to start accepting Bitcoin and has millions in Bitcoins in reserve somewhere, in their online banking network? Well, if the bitcoins they kept on hand for customer receivables got hacked and the millions worth of Bitcoins get stolen somehow, then there's no way for eBay to recover the funds. From my understanding, once a bitcoin passcode/identifier code is gone, it's gone for good, with no real hope of tracking or recovery. At least with cash, someone has to break in and physically steal something from you. With bitcoins, they merely need to steal a string of digital codes, all from the convenience of their own homes.

Ultimately, I think people like to have tangible possession of their assets, being that possession is nine-tenths of the law. Although the crypto-currency works well in transactions where you want some form of ultimate privacy, it doesn't seem feasible to run an entire economy with it. They say its encryption is un-hack-able, but I tend to believe where there's a will there's a way. And with that much money at stake, someone might just get ambitious and try to crack the whole thing wide open. Never forget, there are parts of the government with ridiculous supercomputers out there; so if they wanted to crack it, they could. Then, all that money is virtually useless.

START-UP FEVER

Why we build, the economy of individualism

First and foremost, I want to make it clear that I don't propose to be an expert in anything, except in perhaps determination—or obstinacy depending on how you look at it. If you knew me personally, you might even say some of my business decisions have been downright foolish; to which I would have to admit, I'm guilty as charged. Yet, those faulty business happenings ended up leading me to a much more meaningful form of existence than I ever could have imagined at the outset. Luckily for me, I didn't suffer through all that bad karma and poor planning for nothing. All of my failures helped me to get rid of the malignant and destructive energies within my shadow self. There were many useless parts of my nature that needed to be blown sky high.

During my first business, Catering Promoters, I had a hard time stringing together four straight working hours. I'm not sure if it was my spiritual ADD or my inherent inbuilt aversion to hard work, but whatever it was prevented me from getting things done in an efficient and expedient manner. I would literally spend large swaths of time staring at my computer and just dreading the phone calls I would have to make later that day. In retrospect, it's easy to say that perhaps those businesses were just not a source of passion for me; but I think there were other subconscious problems beyond that, of which I had to overcome as well. Having the focus level of a gnat doesn't help when you have to self-motivate. Later on, I figured out that it is an absolute necessity to have an office outside of your home space when possible, as it just breeds a sense of purpose and focus. I also found my chanting practice very effective for developing mental clarity and detail-oriented endurance.

In the beginning of Catering Promoters, there was an element of excitement in it for me, as I was forced to break into secure high-end office buildings to deliver literature for my restaurant clients, guerilla style. Once I had created stability within that business, I figured out the way to do it was via cold calling, an activity I absolutely deplore. Hence, I eventually had to pack up shop and move on to something more my style. An ultimately difficult decision, as I was fiscally ill-prepared to make such a dramatic leap into the world of digital media.

At the same time, I also realized that I had not done my clients justice. They had effectively trusted me with their marketing dollars (albeit in small amounts) and I had let a few of them down. It was actually sad to me looking back that I didn't really truly value their money as I did my own. I just thought that I had earned it by selling them on my initial program and that my follow-through was some kind of bonus for them. Even though I didn't come from money in any regard, I still had embraced some of the societally degenerative entitlement mentality. Perhaps it was all the rich brats that were at school; whatever the case, this whole way of thinking had to go. And slowly but surely I started to understand how utterly important it was that I go the extra mile for each and every one of my clients. I guess I was around 21 or 22 at the time, but I feel like I should have known better—being that I had already been in the working world for 8 years at that point.

The decision to leave my Catering Promoters venture was a difficult one, as it meant more fiscal insecurity for me in the short term, with no clear short-term cash flow in sight. I eventually decided to pursue a more cutting-edge style of business: it ended up being a project that would face much more market resistance than my other sales-based model had.

Still, all difficulties aside, by allowing the deconstructive model to run its course in my life, it helped me to transform my bad work habits into a marketable skill set—which, in turn, enabled me to make steady progress toward my goals. Sadly, startup progress can be painfully slow, especially at the outset. Startups can be tricky when you don't know your market and your market doesn't know you.

If there is anything that starting at rock bottom will teach you, it's a good bit of patience. As it turns out, life doesn't work on my timetable; it generally has its own plans. Success happens for its own reasons and in tune with its own motives. Sometimes it's dumb luck; and sometimes it is 30 years of trial and error. But, I have never met an honest entrepreneur who has given economic autonomy an honest shot—and has not eventually had some degree of success. In my experience, it has more to do with the inner preparation in many cases, as success can be a dangerous Molotov cocktail in ignorant hands. You have to prepare to wield your power responsibly, lest you become another sad VH1 Behind the Music story. Luckily, the Dao also has a profound sense of humor, for the man who laughs at himself has much to laugh about. Conversely, if you don't fully integrate, or destroy your self-destructive tendencies, then they will hunt you down eventually—effectively cutting you down in your prime.

For years, people told me that I would be better off getting a day job—perhaps by finding a job that utilizes my creative potential in middle management somewhere. Other people said governmental jobs with good pensions would be a better plan, like being a cop or a firefighter. Yet, in my eyes, the search for security is an elusive one, as change is the only constant in our universe. Truth be told, I have never worked for a company that totally coincided with the unique vision I have for my life; and I doubt such a company exists. For I feel I have a very different take on what economic development should consist of on this planet. Many see things as they are, while I try to see them as they might be.

Any diehard entrepreneur will tell you that working for another company long term is not an option. A true entrepreneur will try damn near anything to make their vision a reality, as they know deep down that no job will ever embrace you as an individual—only a true vocation can do that. A true entrepreneur also knows that as difficult as life can be, nothing is impossible. Sadly, no one really tells you how much patience, pragmatism, and planning is required to build dreams. Entrepreneurship requires that you create deep, inwardly rooted, stability in your life so that the small things don't get to you anymore.

In the early days, most of your time will be spent pulling up weeds and digging out the roots of your own failure. Soon enough, your soul will start to sprout leaves and you will get to see some of the fruits of your labor. Anybody can jumpstart a car; but if the battery can't hold a charge, then they won't be getting very far down the road. These get-rich-quick jackasses fall into the previous category. Easy come easy go: if you want lasting stability, most of the time you have to bleed for it. This much I can attest to. Obviously, some will luck out, but I have only seen that a handful of times. Mostly, these folks constitute that rare group, who know their true purpose from the start; and become masters at listening to their intuition.

Now, I don't actually recommend the entrepreneurial lifestyle for everyone, as many people will end up giving up due to the pressure. The road to success isn't really a road; it's actually a long series of ditches you have to crawl out of. Anyone who tells you different hasn't yet had his or her trust fund revoked!

All jesting aside, many people who start out to try and establish fiscal self-sufficiency won't be able to weather the psychological storms that come with the territory. Since everything in this universe is a microcosm of the macrocosm, any time you try to change something for the better in the external world a similar shift will need to take place in your internal psychological sphere to make it a reality.

For me, it took a long sojourn into the unlikely realms of alternative healing before I was really ready to find my vocation. Not to say this is the correct route for everyone, quite the opposite. I think that every being in nature finds their healing in their own unique way. I encourage you to follow your heart, your morality, and your intuition: these are three things that will never let you down. They will guide you toward what is required for your further spiritual development; and also help you to get you navigate this strange and stressful place known as Earth. My quest was fraught with many uncomfortable internal changes; so don't expect all of your friends to come along for the ride. Not everyone wants to sign up for a journey fraught with such internal suffering. Nor do I expect the masses to have the patience or courage to vanquish their internal demons, one by one.

The smart startup gets psychologically prepared at the outset, knowing that time after time storms will show up on your doorstep like the big bad wolf trying to blow your fiscal house down. Anything you cling tightly to will eventually evade your grasp. Ultimately, we always need to be prepared to part ways and go it alone, as no friendship or business lasts forever. If you aren't able to be a lone wolf if need be, then you are always in danger of being compromised. Attachment to wealth, or anything of the sort, creates spiritual liabilities, so to speak. The only man who can lose something is the man who thinks he gained something external to begin with. The only treasures we retain long term are internal. Too much decadence, hubris, and codependency creates a slovenly soul.

People who have long-standing family responsibilities would do well to exercise caution when pursuing entrepreneurial life. Endangering your family's welfare for the sake of egotistical business aggrandizement is never recommended. I have seen this risk taken with mixed results. We must remember that, ultimately, no good man's dream is ever forgotten and children have their own unique way of manifesting things; thereby, helping their parents to find success. I firmly believe that as stupid as parents can be, children will always be provided for just like all of the other creatures in the universe. Never give up on your dreams, just make sure that that timing makes sense for you. It's always good to check in with your inner spiritual conscience, astrologer, spiritual guide, or financial planner to garner additional insights. Having an educated opinion is always beneficial before the outset of your endeavor, as well as working within the natural rhythms of nature and time.

START-UP FEVER

The Blue Pill

Had I realized how much personal strife was required in starting a business at the outset, perhaps I would have just taken a desk job somewhere and sold out to the man. That's the trick; because on the outside, entrepreneurship looks like an easier way of life. Alas, selling out is not in my blood. I was not only born a fighter, but I am also a glutton for punishment. If there is a hill to climb, I will find the strongest climber in the region and give him my race badge. Again, I jest, but perseverance never used to be my strong suit. It was another hydra I had to grapple with in order to make progress. Eight rounds in the octagon with a day planner, spreadsheets, and an accountant can make you feel like a little less of a man; that's all I'm going to say on that.

Another one of my objectives in writing this book was to be able to get through to the ADD generation: a misunderstood generation with the attention span of a gnat. Sadly, most of them stopped reading this at the table of contents and proceeded to light up a joint; so, if you have made it this far, my hat goes off to you. There's still hope! I truly feel that if our up-and-coming, duly insubordinate, youth knew that they didn't have to just attend to one career for the rest of their lives they might be inspired to try a little bit of everything. They might start to take joy in getting their hands dirty, while taking names of the corporations that need to be taken down a peg or two in the process. There will always be enough middle managers in the world—and never enough leaders. Why not try something new and different while you're young? The modern world could always use another healthy dose of idiosyncratic business acumen. If you are blessed enough to be young and are actually interested in reading or studying things you love, then you are the best hope this world has to mount a theological resistance to the bullshit and bureaucracy which abounds. It is only through willful ignorance that the world has become this fragmented escapist dystopia. People who are constantly informing themselves about the world surrounding them are rarely deceived.

If you know anything about the alternative research community, you probably realize that the Silicon Valley gurus are actually hoping that building an army of robots to be their slaves—along with plugging their minds into computers to make themselves digital gods. If that seems logical, then apparently I need to go live on an island alone somewhere; that sounds too coo-coo for Co-Co Puffs for me. I mean does the movie *The Matrix* or *Blade Runner* ring any bells to anyone? Every type of perversion of the human spirit has been committed in the name of keeping people ignorant and scared. The most dangerous man alive is the man who truly knows himself. I wouldn't labor to be trite enough to say that knowledge is resistance, but I will say that inner vision is a good start.

Many people along the way have called me crazy, a loser, a broke ass, a dreamer, or many other things that would discourage the average chap from his pursuits. Yet, for me, the joy has always been in the challenge. If you're starting a business just for the money, you will be sorely disappointed time and again when the money just never seems like enough—and ultimate satisfaction proves elusive. Anything we want, we must first give up on; such is the nature of the universe. I don't want to convey this in some sort of hippie, new-age, context, but in a pragmatic sense, as I feel people can handle the truth.

"I am a firm believer in the people. If given the truth, they can be depended upon to meet any national crisis. The great point is to bring them the real facts." —Abraham Lincoln

I think we're all old enough to stop the sugar coating and to get down to brass tacks; if you want some new-age fluff, I'm sure I could dig up some old Care Bears episodes for you and we can all have a big hug underneath a rainbow of gumdrops. Just shoot me an email, we can make that happen; and remember, as the Lego movie says: "everything is cool when your part of a team." I tried the whole yoga approach; but sooner or later, I had to get real and wake up. After all of that Ra-Ra yoga nonsense, I came to realize that new agers just want to put you up on a pedestal so they can take your money and give you some surface-level feel-good happiness. This yoga, hippy, happiness is destined to fade as humanity realizes that these things mostly run skin deep. We have to find our own path to happiness within.

Zero to Hero

One of my favorite stories of all time is about the sixty-year-old South African music sensation "Rodriguez." After having his album flop in Motown during the 60s, and being totally unknown to the Western world for 30 years, a man's dream of being a worldwide music sensation finally came true. It just so happened that his music sold tens of thousands of copies in South Africa and he was a folk hero during the Apartheid revolution. Sadly, he was never recognized from 1960-1992 because it was rumored that he had died. His reemergence was made possible due to a South African researcher who began digging and, eventually, found out that Rodriguez was still alive and well—and living in Detroit. He was working construction and barely eking by in a less-than-desirable neighborhood. I'm sure many of you have seen the documentary, but it's truly one of the most heartwarming underdog stories of all time. The documentary is called *Sugarman* for those of you who want to watch it. Truly, this man's story is one of the most remarkable tales to ever grace the Earth. If you don't think anything is possible after watching that, I don't know what to tell you.

Now, obviously, there will be those amongst us who just have that one thing they are called to do in life; and hell or high water, that's all that they will do for the entirety of their lives. And to those people I say: congratulations! You should feel fortunate because that kind of existence can be a serious blessing; many people have that insanely passionate calling to do that one thing. Even though many of you out there may have that type of calling as well, sometimes subconscious impediments can cause you to fear your inherent abilities. This is something I certainly struggled with on a personal level. To embrace your true power is a scary thing, as it means you will start to be judged to a greater extent by the world at-large; and who really likes to be judged on an abject level? So, what if it takes you until later in my life to do your most fulfilling work? Ultimately, the existence of time is debatable—and who are we really trying to impress. Remember the words of Lao Tzu: "Nature never rushes, yet everything gets accomplished." Some people are just meant to shine earlier in life. Apparently, I wanted to be the horse that breaks late in the race.

Out of virtue of necessity I had to do many other things to build up the confidence in myself to the point where I would subconsciously allow myself to start doing what I really wanted to do all along. Honestly, I wouldn't wish the profound turbulence of my quest on anyone except the fiercest and most humble of entrepreneurs, as it was no picnic. Nor will my life ever be "easy." Only when you have tasted defeat can you realize how much victory truly means—and how hollow it can seem if done for the wrong reasons. Without a personal philosophy and existential determination to achieve something beyond your own sphere of existence, and material acquisitiveness, you will never amount to much.

Ch. 1
Purpose-Based Economics

F ast forward to 2014, little did I realize how much work being a real-life entrepreneur would entail. Other books will tell you harrowing tales of massive corporate success against all odds, of which I know there are many cases. But it's more important to deal with crowdfunding on a purpose level, as we are working with a phenomenon which is still in its infancy stages. And right now, I see it as more important to steer the ship in a virtuous direction and not worry about all of the waves or storms that might befall the ship during its journey; where the ultimate destination of our crowdfunding journey lands is anyone's guess.

But I do know that you don't have to have much money to start a business; and the fact is that almost all of my ventures have been started with almost no upfront capital. Pragmatically speaking, life always works on its own terms. Although you may not be able to change your life all the time, your life will always change you. At any point, you may be forced to leave everything you have ever worked for, and built upon, and be okay with it. I know this, as I have had to leave several profitable businesses that took me years to establish. I also know many other entrepreneurs who have faced similar circumstances.

If you live your whole life attempting to build some form of external fortress to shield yourself from the vagaries of life, you're in for an unpleasant awakening. No business will ever give you some form of supreme control over life. Many times, these structures people have built to shield themselves have no choice but to come crashing down. We all remember my good friend Humpty Dumpty, that poor son of a gun is still walking around on crutches. All the king's horses, and all the king's men didn't do much for him. Hell, he couldn't even get on disability. The world just isn't fair sometimes—especially when you're an egg who is trying to scale a large wall! Learn from our good friend Mr. Dumpty! Don't climb walls when you're a giant egg; man, it probably won't work out.

But in all seriousness, stability is hard to come by in this world because as it turns out, we live in a very transient dimension. Quantum scientists and day-trippers alike seem to agree that things are not as solid as they might appear. Many different spiritual leaders from time eternal have preached that this world consists of little more than shadows and dust. Having had many of my own dreams crash and burn in front of my eyes, I would have to agree that certainty in the business world is an elusive phantasmagoria. Many times, stability in the business world comes artificially through the use of force or corruption. This is how the dark side operates. The visionaries in the business world are willing to compete via skill, not by coercion, and certainly not by abject force. Now, the threat of force may be implied in a defensive way, but not as the unwarranted aggressor. Destroying another virtuous man's dream is an abhorrent idea to a true vocationalist. Corporate takedowns should be looked at like the murder of a dream, not a legal payday like a lesser man would view it.

Now, I did not write this book for the aspiring Bill Gates or Donald Trump; and that's for good reason. I myself also had dreams of fame and fortune at the outset of my quest; but, generally speaking, I have found it much less emotionally taxing to aim for personal growth, then for monetary gain. This world is not meant to be "owned" in a monetary sense; this world is meant to be experienced. We can always guarantee ourselves personal growth; where with monetary reward, there are no such assurances. Simply put: I view human beings as temporary visitors on this plane of existence. As such, we do not "own" the earth"; if anything, it's quite the opposite. Any inclinations toward becoming a "gatekeeper" for others lives should be thought about long and hard.

On the darker side, many of the more controlling entrepreneurs use their money as a shield to prevent them from emotionally participating in their own lives. Usually, these people had very emotionless upbringings where they were only rewarded on a very conditional basis by their parents—or parental figures. This much fractured cycle then gets repeated in the outside world, much to the chagrin of those working for these unscrupulous characters. Their money also serves as a way to solicit continual approval, no matter how morally questionable their actions may or not be.

Many of these hyper-extrovert-overachiever types feel that the world would sink without their guidance; and perhaps their role is quite necessary as some form of unseen karmic balancing. But, I have a feeling that the world would get along just fine without one more global empire. We have quite enough of those. As we all know, the quest to take over the world is as old as mankind itself. If Alexander the Great and Genghis Kahn failed, so too shall the current batch of megalomaniacal crazies fail in their vain attempt to ensnare the world for their own unsavory purposes.

I only mention this in an effort to realize that the dichotomy of benevolent and monovalent entrepreneurial minds does exist—and will continue to exist. So, it is up to us to choose the higher path toward harmony for our fellow humans. Money made at the expense of others has failed to create true value in the world. This is one of the major mythos of warfare: it's good for the economy and that it breeds innovation. This type of thinking is also aberrant, as warfare breeds nothing but malcontent and destruction. Even if it is necessary on some levels, it should never be looked at as a positive thing in the world; it should always be a last resort and not a childish game.

Deep down—as one of my mentors, Michael Tsarion has pointed out—the negative use of technology represents little more than mankind's futile attempt to rival the divine abilities of creation found within nature. I can assure you that whatever gadget mankind invents, nature has already beaten us to the punch. To think you can outwit nature, or that you can control nature, is a blatant fallacy. This mentality just leads to more walls and fewer windows.

Obviously, I am painting with a broad brush here, but I only offer warning so that you can avoid a lifestyle built upon some unquenchable void of monetary acquisition, or implied control. Who would want to be a 24/7 workaholic anyways? I think deep down everyone realizes that they need a little time alone to contemplate their deeper self, along with the mysteries of life. Even though many corporate moguls start out with noble intentions, it's hard to maintain purity of intent without cultivating strong spiritual discipline.

Now, if you want to give world domination a shot, be my guest. But thousands upon thousands of case studies of famous personages will soon show you that money cannot buy happiness. Having too much of anything will always make you a target, as it represents nature's way of trying to restore balance. Yet the man with just enough is okay with everyone; he is generous with everyone around him and, most of all, he is generous with himself. The best we may do in this world is to live a life that is in harmony with the people, places, and nature that is all around us.

Granted, on the opposite end of the spectrum I know a good amount of very wealthy entrepreneurs who are actually amazingly benevolent pioneers, true innovators who worked their way from the ground up. These people generally have a deep appreciation of everything they have ever earned, which effectively translates into a supremely generous monetary outlook. These types of individuals are able to create massive structural reforms within society, as well as amass wealth, which can contribute to the beautification of cities and contribute to artistic creations. Minds such as this are truly able to help others help themselves.

The truly benevolent creative individual is a beautiful thing to behold. In my experience, the happiest people are those who maintain an appreciation for the small things; as the small joys in life will always exist, in good times or in bad. The humble ones around us can show us where the true beauty of life lives.

START-UP FEVER

A spiritually minded entrepreneur works because he knows that there is a better way for the business world to function, which would allow more people to reach their true potential. By sharing their unique vocation with the world, they know that they are slowly, but surely, changing things for the better. They realize that the businesses they create allow people better opportunities to live an inspired and productive lifestyle. They know that their businesses will naturally generate harmony out in the world. In essence, the vision for their vocation generally goes way beyond themselves. The spiritually minded entrepreneurs deeply connected sense of self stems from a deep appreciation for their innately creative nature. The truly inwardly directed person sees the need to direct others as a duty, but takes no pleasure in controlling other people's actions or exacting cruel work practices.

Nature's action in the world is entirely idiosyncratic, spontaneously creating millions of useful solutions a second. Somehow, nature accomplishes this all without the use of board meetings or uniforms. Can you imagine that? When is the last time your dog complained about not having enough time? My point exactly! In my estimation, the entrepreneurial community has much to learn from nature and should view it as a solid go-to for inspiration on sustainable practices. Nature has existed for eons, while modern civilization only represents a fraction of that timeline. Even with the massive amounts of human development out in the world. I bet that only ten to fifteen percent of the land mass actually contains some form of modern structure. That leaves eighty-five to ninety percent of the earth that naturally reproduces itself. No rebar or concrete foundations are required. Nature represents a constant cycle of regeneration for which we should be supremely grateful.

I mention the need for patience, as I know that budding entrepreneurs can be some of the most impatient people on earth—especially since everyone has been programmed to think that getting rich quick is a good plan. When, in fact, getting rich quick can be a recipe for disaster. Just look at Lindsay Lohan or Justin Bieber, teens with too much money and not enough life experience; they are not exactly sterling role models in the emotional or spiritual spheres. Not to mention the fact that ninety percent of lottery winners go broke within five years of getting their cash. Maybe we should be talking to people like this and asking them if getting rich quick was a blessing or a curse. That is, if you can find one sober enough to hold a sentence together.

Liftoff

The ultra-narcissistic ego-freak lifestyle is a trite routine that has been played out in countless instances in the past, so why beat that dead horse? I have come to understand during my work in the spiritual spheres that working for the sake of work can constitute a form of existential avoidance. This is a rookie mistake that will retard your internal development, which I believe is the prime directive of our species.

If you have a loving family, good friends, a comfortable dwelling, a fulfilling job, then what else do you really need? My aim is to show you how to succeed from humble beginnings and spiritually downtrodden surroundings. You won't necessarily take over the world, but you will be happy! The only true certainties I have found in life are few and far between, but I do know that we are given a chance to find harmony within ourselves. Although the world is perpetually turning in circles, that doesn't mean that we need to run in circles to as well. I can assure you that the world does enough spinning for the lot of us. We are all flying through outer space at 108,000 km per hour on a living, thinking, and breathing spaceship known as Earth. If you think you are somehow capable of captaining this ship solo, you're sorely mistaken.

Perhaps the earth is just one big atom that's spinning its way back home. Or perhaps it's just a snow globe, inside another snow globe, inside another snow globe. If humans and animals have "work to do," it would serve to reason that the earth also has a vocation of its own. It is anyone's guess where in the universe we actually are, but we should always remember that we do not have the spiritual right to control anything other than ourselves. So, keep your hands and your thoughts inside the vehicle as we prepare for a crowdfunding takeoff!

We have fantabulous noodles between our ears than can accomplish seemingly impossible feats. We need to learn how to use this magnificent tool in a way that brings harmony. When you can learn to be happy living in the universe within you, you can be happy anytime and at any place; and the external world of chaos loses its power over you. Quantum science has continually pointed toward the fact that our internal world might just be just as real as our external one. I doubt that anyone would argue the fact that many of the greatest things in the world started out as ideas first. So something important must be going on in that space between your ears!

Corporations: The Modern Day Castles

Even though life may become difficult at times, that by no means gives us the right to use business to shield us from the human experience of emotionality. When you look at the emotional disconnection of the modern business world from a deeper level, you start to realize that corporations can also represent a form of emotional shielding as well. Corporate America can be a very emotionally toxic place. Instead of teaching our workforce how to deal effectively with their own emotional reactions appropriately, we have chosen to teach them how to shut down—all in the name of productivity; a cycle that will repeat itself ad infinitum until we realize that there is a problem.

Workplaces can become breeding grounds for ice-cold emotionless interactions. Obviously, business is different from personal life, but people need to know how to deal with emotions in their off-time if they are going to be successful and emotionally healthy in the long haul. Again, I'm not trying to shove this stuff down any employee's throat, but perhaps sending out daily YouTube videos that deal with these deeper issues could be of value –along with setting aside time for meditation, tai chi, nature outings, qi gong, or other decompression modalities.

Again, I'm a pragmatist and I understand that business is business on many levels. But if we don't have some form of healthy emotional release for the workforce, we will just have to deal with another crop of narcissistic sociopaths—a crop that will breed more economic instability as this control-freak-dominant-businessman shtick constitutes a vain cry for help.

Respect!

At outset of most of my ventures, I only had a few hundred dollars and a dream. As Jim Rome said, "The same wind blows upon us all," and it's up to us to use the current societal circumstances to our advantage. Keeping these types of principles in mind, I was determined to persevere whatever the economic obstacles were. This bootstrap mentality is eventually how I discovered the majesty of crowdfunding and the Groupon marketing mechanism—vehicles that allow you to start any business with almost no money down and a good chance of success. Like one of my mentors used to say, "My teachings are a salad bar. Take what you want. Leave the rest behind." I feel like the area of spiritually based economics is one that has barely been scratched upon in modern literature. The books that have addressed it have done so in a very airy-fairy new-age kind of way. Setting people up for failure more times than not, these books pander to people looking for some type of future economic utopia—which will probably never exist in our lifetime. Or they show people how to build their economic dream house, but fail to tell them that they first need to demolish that shitty psychic trailer park that's standing in the way of construction.

Real life can get ugly and when it does, I want people to be prepared—physically, psychologically, spiritually, and monetarily. I want all my fellow humans to be able to reach their own maximum potential during their lifetime; and for many of us that requires making some coin along the way. I'm too young to write my memoir and, ultimately, I've been beaten up by life too much to be spewing some ultra-positivist corporate hoorah nonsense. There are plenty of utopia-based life coaches that can regurgitate such slogans in my absence. I just want people to get real about their lives and realize that nine times out of ten, you have to readjust your plans as you go. The secret to entrepreneurial life lies in giving it 110 percent every day; strangely, I have found that hard work actually helps things go smoother many times. It's a half effort that leaves you paddling upstream.

So, if you want to be The Grand Puba, The Big Kahuna, Boss Hog, The Big Noise, The Head Honcho, The Big Cheese, or The Man who draws a lot of water, then you will have to learn how to earn respect. People will rarely do good work for someone they don't respect, let alone someone for whom they don't feel has their best interests at heart. Needless to say, without teamwork your business will not get very far. Unless you're a freelance artist who just needs tons of creative solitude, you will probably have to interact with coworkers or the public in some capacity; neither of these two groups is easily impressed. True self-respect is definitely one of the most fundamental building blocks of success. Earning the respect of others ultimately leads back to trusting our intuition. These are the tools needed to develop a vision that expands past your own limited sphere of influence and beyond where you think your vocational life could possibly take you. Do you think Elvis ever envisioned himself playing music to stadiums full of people when no such feat had ever been accomplished? Perhaps he did; or perhaps his quest was just larger than he could have ever fathomed.

All possibilities are only open to the man who is open to all possibilities. If you want to find the perfect entrepreneur, you should look for someone who been beaten down by life—a person who has had to rebuild his or her life from scratch a time or two. These are the types of people who will lead you toward the real meaning behind it all. What lies beyond the entire rat race is in inherent quest for selfhood—a quest to acquire an indestructible virtuousness that you will carry with you past this life and beyond. So take your time, for although you may be smart, the hardest-working people know that sustainable success involves a gradual ascent. We have all heard the stories of entrepreneurs having huge projects go bust and having to rebuild from the rubble. Throughout life, most people will spend 30%-40% of their waking life working, so why not roam the professional spheres in search of greener pastures? The grass may not be greener on the other side, but it's a hell of a lot of fun jumping over fences while running from the police! You didn't think entrepreneurship was without risk, did you? Obviously, you will have to make some tough leadership decisions, so let your morality be your guide!

Technology, for better, or worse, till death do us part!

One of my favorite stand-up comedy bits of all time is when George Carlin is ranting about everyone's incessant need to take pictures or to shoot video to preserve precious moments in their life. At the end of the rant he laments: "Does anyone just take the time and take a few minutes to just take in the moment anymore? To take two seconds to use your own mind to create the memory instead of having fifty thousand little snapshots to pretend like you were enjoying yourself?" I, for one, know that the mind can retain images with incredible clarity; I went to the Grand Canyon when I was 8 and I can still see that image in my mind like it was yesterday. No stupid techno gadget necessary. With any luck, the image will be with me until the day I die. I would have a hard time saying that such immortal memories are possible via some flash drive or some HD video camera. Can they recount how the wind swept over your arms? Can the video recall how it smelled that day? Can the picture show you how the reflections of the light created sweat on your brow? I think not.

To counterpoint this hyper-tech future, I also see a group of young entrepreneurs emerging that have little tolerance for the spiritually neglectful ideals of corporations past. These kids have a rough go, growing up in broken homes with both parents working 40-50 hours a week—leaving the kids to raise themselves on a steady diet of internet and TV. By the time they get to high school, they have been introduced to more sex, drugs, and rap than you can shake a stick at. Hence, they are trying to get their lives straightened out, as to not have to repeat the unsustainable family life that their parents' leaderless generation created. I know this to be true because I am one of those kids. One who said to hell with this system and set out to rebuild a sense of true prosperity in society.

Isn't it ironic that many of those free love hippies have now adopted methodologies of the bureaucratic oppressors that they were supposedly rebelling against? I guess it was just a matter of time before the slave wanted to become the master…free love, my ass! All those listless potheads now just want a free ride from the system—at the expense of their children no less. I think the actions of dictatorial monarchies throughout history should make it clear that governments do not solve problems for people; they create them. If you want anything for free from a government, you are delusional; governments are not meant to be of service, they are meant for control. If you want my opinion, I believe that entrepreneurs should strive for as little government contact as possible. The less attention you pay to these vipers, the better off you will be. Trying to change the world via traditional governmental means is a fool's task; you're much better off changing yourself and thereby changing the world in a subtle, but much more powerful, way.

Freedom comes organically from the people or, sometimes, in the extremely rare instance of moral and noble national leadership. Whatever the case, the modern broken-home scenario is quickly killing what little morality was left in this country; and organized religion and governmental structures have been hard at work killing the rest. Again, if you want true change, it's going to have to come from within; the outside world in its current state of psychological disrepair is a very unstable place. We need to be psychically armed to the teeth and ready for anything. The battles of the 22nd century and beyond will be fought in the mind!

Ch. 2

The Time to Strike...

As men wiser than me will inevitably tell you, timing is everything; and without the right timing, you will be bereft of any long-term gain. Anyone who has ever tried to score a date with most attractive person in their school will tell you: there is nothing valuable about being the eager beaver. There's always a time to strike; but if you put your cards on the table too soon, there's no way to come away a big winner. Sometimes, you must be patient and wait for your time to swoop in. I do know that the time for planning your own business is now, as this is the best opportunity for a semi-unregulated crowd-fund that you will ever have. You can currently get your unique idea out to the masses within a very short timeframe and with very big possible results, given proper execution. Currently, the mega-conglomerates are so busy trying to set up rigged markets that they are leaving their economic defenses wide open—leaving plenty of market-share to be gobbled up by local small businesses. The weak always overcome the strong; it's only a matter of time.

Corporate real estate will soon go bust, the evidence of which is all around you. One only need look around to realize that the vacancy rate in these strip malls and corporate mega-complexes is very high. Many of these buildings must run at occupancy for over a decade to pay off the initial construction cost. Without tenants, people can't pay rent. That being the case, there will be a lot of entrepreneurial market-share left to be gobbled up in those sectors as well. How many vacant strip malls will people have to abandon before creative small business opportunities emerge in their wake? The urban sprawl can't go on forever in its current wasteful manner. At some point, you will be able to start talking to these property owners and getting reduced rent in exchange for equity in your startup; either that or perhaps townships will start offering reduced rent and lower taxes to small businesses, who currently pay the highest taxes across the board.

> "Anita Durst—the iconoclastic artist granddaughter of controversy-addled Time Square real estate developer Seymour Durst—founded the nonprofit organization Chashama in 1995 to foster a relationship between owners of underused real estate and the city's emerging artists. Here's how Chashama's model works: building owners come to Chashama when they have properties they're having trouble renting. Chashama rents the property itself—generally at a discounted price on a month-to-month basis—and then offers the space to an artist who has an idea for an installation in the space." www.thirteen.org/metrofocus/2011/10/no-vacancy-turning-empty-spaces-into-cultural-pop-ups/

These types of alternative methods of business creation will become extremely handy in tight markets where room for error is small. Even internet-based businesses can still utilize this model for warehousing, production space, or staging. In all honesty, this large glut of open space may come to represent a mass resettling of the West in a sense. I feel like whoever is able to quickly monetize this will be in high demand. Really, the possibilities are endless.

Where there's a will there's a way; and crowdfunding will have a large bearing on the mega-banks not being able to totally shut down the small business sector. I look at crowdfunding as a way to vote with your dollars. It puts the entrepreneur front and center, instead of education levels or some form of popularity contest. Amongst other markets that are showing signs of life, sustainable farming isn't a bad one either; people will definitely have more interest in starting small farms as the weather patterns continue to worsen in the "bread basket" of America. Quality food might be shorter in supply. I can only hope that somehow local organic farmers are able to adequately harness this energy for their own purposes as well— helping to bring more profitability to small local farming.

Overall, I equate this to capitalism getting another fair shake here in America. Obviously nothing is easy, but even very unconventional businesses have had massive success utilizing these micro-loan mechanisms. No matter what anyone says: when it comes to business, I feel like Americans will always have something inventive up their sleeves in times of crisis. The innovation of companies like, GoPro, MailChimp, Uber, Lyft, and Waze continually amazes me. On one level, I doubt that anyone in big business really saw crowdfunding coming, as they continue to be very slow to respond to this emerging force. Again, this won't last more than a handful of years, as people come to realize that they must adapt or else...

Sadly, it's been hard to get lots of positive press for the crowdfunding boom as other areas of the economy have been so lackluster in growth that they are gobbling up much of the news cycle. Anyone who doesn't think that this country is going through a full-blown depression has not looked at the hard numbers; and, sadly, it seems that it will have to get a bit worse before it gets better. Again, I'm not a pessimist, as everyone is capable of prosperity whatever the economic circumstances. You just have to have enough internal fortitude to weather the psychological storm and not lose your marbles during the low times.

During great upheaval, great changes in fortune can occur, for better and for worse. We should just aim to go with the flow and be on the good end of this economic "downturn." Any real entrepreneur worth their salt knows that their wealth comes from within; having things externally is just a representation of that. Anyone who has read "Atlas Shrugged" knows that men of purpose will always be able to create a better way of life that is in harmony with current global trends...

> "Productiveness is your acceptance of morality, your recognition of the fact that you choose to live—that productive work is the process by which man's consciousness controls his existence, a constant process of acquiring knowledge and shaping matter to fit one's purpose, of translating an idea into physical form, of remaking the earth in the image of one's values--that all work is creative

work if done by a thinking mind, and no work is creative if done by a blank who repeats in uncritical stupor a routine he has learned from others—that your work is yours to choose, and the choice is as wide as your mind, that nothing more is possible to you and nothing less is human—that to cheat your way into a job bigger than your mind can handle is to become a fear-corroded ape on borrowed motions and borrowed time, and to settle down into a job that requires less than your mind's full capacity is to cut your motor and sentence yourself to another kind of motion: decay—that your work is the process of achieving your values, and to lose your ambition for values is to lose your ambition to live—that your body is a machine, but your mind is its driver, and you must drive as far as your mind will take you, with achievement as the goal of your road—that the man who has no purpose is a machine that coasts downhill at the mercy of any boulder to crash in the first chance ditch, that the man who stifles his mind is a stalled machine slowly going to rust, that the man who lets a leader prescribe his course is a wreck being towed to the scrap heap, and the man who makes another man his goal is a hitchhiker no driver should ever pick up—that your work is the purpose of your life, and you must speed past any killer who assumes the right to stop you, that any value you might find outside your work, any other loyalty or love, can be only travelers you choose to share your journey and must be travelers going on their own power in the same direction." —Ayn Rand, *Atlas Shrugged*

Step by Step

Steps to a successful startup have been beat to death in other texts; and I don't intend to beat a dead horse with this book. Simply put: there's a few things you should do before you can really consider a venture viable. I think a lot of people also overthink things to the point where they say, "Oh, I could never do that." One of my favorite quotes of all time is: "I have never begun an adventure for which I was adequately prepared." So, don't sweat the small stuff you can learn as you go along; many small businesses are a moving target and you won't be able to plan for everything. As Murphy's law states: if it can go wrong, it generally will. So, we just have to go out there and do the best that we can. But for those of you that would like a concise list of my ultra-low budget bootstrapping techniques, here you are....

Business Plan

Yes, this means crunching a few numbers and making sure you can turn a profit with your model. Failing to plan is planning to fail. I'm not saying this has to be so airtight that investors can read your 100-page, five-year, plan; but if you don't know what you're going to be doing to build your business next week, that might be an issue. Why do CEOs get paid the big bucks? They get paid the big bucks because they are looking 5, 10, 30 years in the future—assessing industry trends and planning to steer the company away from economic roadblocks. Bob the Janitor gets paid nine an hour because he only has to worry about what he's going to do today. No complex planning involved. So, if big money is if your aim, then you might want to learn how to plan ahead—or at least employ someone else who can. God knows, long-term planning can a boring and sterile subject for the most part; but, honestly, it doesn't have to be. If you're passionate about your business, thinking about your future in that regard should be a fun exercise in productive daydreaming. Check out the book The Lean Startup by Eric Ries for further ideas here as well!

Market Research

This includes time spent assessing the competition and figuring out how viable it will be to sell your product or service at a given price-point. Obviously, there is no need to reinvent the wheel; so, if there's something your competitor does well, take note and incorporate that into your plans. Imitation is the greatest flattery as they say. If you're doing a better job at your company than the competitor is, there is no reason why stealing market-share is something about which to feel bad. There's enough cash to go round. There is nothing new under the sun as they say, so really it's just fine-tuning you're offering and determining what unique qualities your company possesses that will differentiate you from the competition.

Test Marketing

I can't stress how important this one is. I don't know how many times I failed to make this a main priority during my startup process. All I know is that trying to launch a product or service without getting people to buy it is a very risky plan. Sometimes, a novel idea might be too specific; sometimes, an idea is ahead of its time; sometimes, other companies are blocking your market somehow. There are a million and one reasons a product can fail, so making sure you have a good chance at garnering a customer base is essential. Take it from me: if you can't sell your idea to at least one of your Facebook friends, then it's probably not a winner. And if your market is too narrow, then you will have a heck of a time getting your goods or services sold out in the real world. So, please spare yourself the heartache and money by testing it out. Business is hard enough; nothing is more anti-climactic than a failed business launch you have poured your hard-earned nest egg into. If it doesn't have legs, then take it out back and shoot it. Sadly, many businesses seem good in theory, yet fail in practice. There's no need to get discouraged, trial and error is half of the fun! The best revenge isn't always massive success; sometimes, it's about the changes you make in others by putting forth your best effort. As Jim Rome would say: failure is a better teacher than success. Just go with the flow and always do your best, that's how things work out well in the end.

Why would you ever want to start something that was completely untested is beyond me. But, the human ego loves to play tricks on people and make them do completely inane things from time to time. So, before you dive into uncharted waters do yourself a favor: do some testing. It's worth it! I can assure you it won't take a thousand tries. As a side note, if that false god Thomas Edison had been tapped into his own intuitive nature, it wouldn't have taken him 2,000 tries. Those connected directly with their higher self arrive at solutions much faster and, henceforth, are referred to as geniuses. Did Michelangelo have to redo The Sistine Chapel 2,000 times? I think not. He got it right the first time because his spiritual self was alive and kicking; his art was merely a vehicle for the dreams of his higher self.

Publicity

You will also need to develop cool media around the product. You need something pretty catchy or unique to cut through the corporate claptrap to grab people's attention. Figure out a niche and start working on concepts that you think would interest your audience. Sometimes it is price; sometimes it is novelty; sometimes it is catchy marketing—or it could be as simple as a great logo. Whatever the case, you will be glad you did the heavy lifting up front. Nothing is worse than a crowdfunding campaign that has flopped due to the fact no one would even read your email because of crappy marketing. 99designs.com is an invaluable resource for those on a tight budget who need comprehensive marketing materials. Although it basically amounts to glorified outsourcing, 99 designs has the market cornered on design work for your dollar. First, you give them a budget ($300-$2,500), and then hundreds of designers go to work creating the logo/website/ marketing materials of your dreams. Sadly, only the winning designer gets paid. It's also a good play to try and make sure that you're always considering how other potential cross-marketing partners will view your publicity work. Are you positioning yourself as a high-end/low-end/boutique brand or company—and does the type of publicity you are garnering match with that vision? Let's just say Rolex won't be doing any crowdfunding anytime soon, as they are too high-brow for all that.

Street Cred

All I can say on this note is "fake it till you make it." In my experience, you generally have to give things away in the beginning just to get reviews. So, just plan on operating at a minor loss in that respect. No one wants to buy products or services that have not yet been subject to some form of peer review. Think about it: would you buy a new car if there were no reviews about the company who had produced it or prior owners of that particular make? Probably not. Obviously, if you're selling hair combs, it might be a different story; but, for most people, online reviews are essential. Until further notice, Yelp, Google, and Facebook have cornered the marketplace for most online reviews, so do what you can to get those reviews in the door.

Marketing

People go to Yelp/Amazon/Consumer Reports so they don't have to piss away money on below-average products and services. During tight economies, there is always less room for error and chances are that if your product sucks, people will find out quickly. Word travels fast on the internet, as if that's any real surprise. Most important of all: no cross-promotional partner will ever touch you if you don't already have an established online presence—or less than stellar online reviews. They can't put their brand at risk if you don't look extremely viable on paper. They need some proof that their investment in your company is worth a damn. The key is spending plenty of time building a convincing argument for the crowdfunding or online marketing vehicle of your choosing. You have to show potential marketing partners that, without a doubt, your business is the best thing since sliced bread and will sell like hotcakes. If you can't show them that, then you're not ready. When it comes to other branding opportunities, social media presence is king. Bottom line being: the bigger your following, the more you can charge for your services.

You will need to have your website up and looking clean, as well as a public address to do business with since you cannot use a residential with Yelp (I've tried). You will also want to list everything on the other directory sites, such as Google maps and what not. That is kind of Internet SEO 101, but it's still good to note. Also, when you build your site, you always want to try to find a skilled low-cost SEO person to consult with before you construct it. They can give you a good idea regarding your target market and what keywords and site features you will want to include for maximum search engine presence. I can't stress enough that content is king. So, the more the better; obviously, good content is best, but people need to be able to find your businesses footprint easily. And that footprint must represent an overarching theme of staying power.

Money in the Bank

Besides all the legwork, you will either want to have enough money in the bank to float you for the first 3-12 months; or you will want to maintain a day job of some sort to get you by until everything else settles in. You don't want to put all of your eggs in one basket and end up going belly up. Nothing is worse than that feeling. Other than having a solid team of compatriots, nothing lets you rest easier than a few clams in the bank—or a steady flow of income to help you get your business started on the right foot. Trust me, I have quit a job to go solo on a prayer and a dream; and although I did it, it was hell and I lost a good bit of hair in the process. You probably want to try to plan things out a little bit better instead of being as impulsive as I was in the outset of my half-baked adventures in youthful folly.

There is something about being broke that other people can smell; and it's a funk that nobody wants to do business with. It's almost like you are subconsciously telling people that they will lose their money by doing business with you; as the saying goes: it takes money to make money. So, if you can, don't start your business with absolutely nothing in the bank. Again, this isn't an overnight gig; to get good at anything takes a long time. Longer than anyone wants to admit, so I'm here to tell you to plan for the long haul.

Almost to the Starting Line

So, to recap, if I had to start something up on the fly: I would build my product or service; get a website up; get some feedback from friends and family; start looking for cross-promotional partnership opportunities; start building up a Yelp account; start looking into getting some PR attention for a Kickstarter campaign or launch on Groupon. Using this model, I think most non-brick-and-mortar businesses should be able to get started with $500-5000 dollars. This Gen-Y startup model minimizes risk while maximizing output; and allows companies to once and for all leave the whole cost-plus-pricing mechanism in the past. A good thing for our economy, as it presents a way to bring skilled labor, or other unique trades, back into the American workforce.

Once you get rolling, there is usually a bit of time to fine tune the operation as well. There is no need to kill yourself running some sort of blowout sale to get clients in the door when you first get up and running. In that case, a soft opening is a much better plan. If you're not honest about the level of fine-tuning that your project will need, then you're just setting yourself up for a launch disaster. I think we have all heard about tech companies that have launched versions of software that were rife with bugs and as a result were lambasted by customers online—never to regain their pre-launch momentum again.

If you can accomplish these 5 steps, you are well on the way to turning a profit. In a pinch, these can be done in a few weeks—or for a larger business, a few months. Ultimately, just follow your gut. Going against your instincts will always land you in trouble. If you feel like you're ready to go, then you probably are; if you feel like you should wait, then you probably should wait. Seems simple, but many people second guess themselves until they are blue in the face; and in their excitement, they leave their common sense behind. Don't do that! Even if your idea goes up in flames, you will survive to pick up the pieces and try again. In the positivist sense, even though this planet can seem like a bit of a *Groundhog Day* scenario from time to time, at least we get the opportunity to wake up every day and try it again. As I always say, "sleep is for the dead and coffee is for the working." I have made these same business practices work with great results, so I know that you can, too, with a little dedication.

Ch. 3

The Upside of the Downturn

Business of the modern age has become a pretty complicated task, especially if you are considering a startup. There's lots of forms to fill out, investors to glad-hand, and competitors to scout out—all before you make dollar one. Luckily, if we maintain the same course, startups twenty to thirty years in the future will entail far less legwork than the ones of today. In the near future, startups might not require the elaborate amounts of investor deliberation, unholy bank loans, or borrowing from friends and family—as was the standard for generations past. This sweeping change in funding modalities will create a much more transparent (and, hopefully, more moral) business environment. As with any change, it will also have a downside. The owner/investor relationship will also change as the economic engine of micro-funding emerges.

This startup reorientation could go one of two ways: either newfound micro-investors will hold business owners less accountable than the venture capitalists of the past; or, conversely, business owners will be stuck with thousands of smaller level micro-managers. My guess is that it will consist of a bit of both. The great news here is that the level of fiscal transparency should be a great thing for corporate ethics. As well as funding projects that have been too risky or untraditional for the old venture-capitalist, big-bank, funding model to work with. If we bring these financial statements into the open, this should at least inspire discussion on revenue streams and their impact in regards to larger social issues. This level of transparency might throw some for a loop; I know how entrepreneurs value their autonomy. So, it's good to go in prepared, as this is a new variable within the startup scene.

Along with the new shareholder crowdfunding model, which was passed with the recent JOBS act legislation, we have already had many massively successful donation-based startups. With the outright donation model being a major part of crowdfunding, this means that self-accountability becomes a big part of the startup puzzle. It also means that there will be a lot of people dreadfully unprepared to start their own business. A scenario that is daunting for the pioneer and investor alike, but I guess they call it donation for a reason.

Let me reiterate that the future of business will require more transparency and self-accountability—a shocking development compared to the financing practices of today. In the good old days, you would have a few venture capitalists breathing down your neck or a looming bank note; but now, it's up to you to go out there and succeed under your own volition. As has been proven by the mass laziness of our society, self-accountability is a tough thing for many people. So, it will be interesting to see how the donation-model startup pans out long term. Hopefully, prospective donation-based investors are doing their homework and not giving money to armchair champions.

Anyone signing a book or record deal in this modern age is living a bit in the past as far as I am concerned. People are paying 2000% premiums for companies to do things that they could easily accomplish themselves with an effectively educated marketing manager, publicist, and/or brand innovator. Social media is allowing for some incredible viral success for many who know how to leverage their platforms effectively. If you know what you're doing, you can turn that nonsensical YouTube content you produce for fun into a profitable career. Companies are always trying to recreate their brands and they have millions of dollars to put toward making their image more "hip," "nerdy," "cool," "stylish," etc. If you can help them to achieve these aims, then you are in a position to get paid for your efforts. The most innovative crowdfunding entrepreneurial minds I know use this model; and have been at it well before Kickstarter was a twinkling in your browser's eye. Branding and cross-promotional innovation are some of the most powerful tools in today's entrepreneurial arsenal—and worth further investigation for the inquiring mind.

This newfound financing engine will allow us more control over the moral development of our civilization and, hopefully, enable us to bring jobs back to this country by running businesses that require less overhead. As the system stands now, big businesses and governments can do anything they please until otherwise noted by the courts—which they largely control. The current economic system has inspired untold technological developments, while simultaneously subduing the spiritual and moral development of many Americans. By looking at the artistic creations coming out of the small but focused group of

START-UP FEVER

"true artists" still left, it is easy to see that the youth of today is looking for a way out. Crowdfunding is the natural result of just such a universal subconscious request. The mantra of this new entrepreneurial generation is: if there are no fulfilling jobs to be filled, then I will just go out and make my own. This is a philosophy which should be applauded in my view, as it harkens back to the origins of Americana and the reinvention of the American Dream.

Although crowdfunding is an amazing first step in the right direction, it still remains a first step. Much inner determination will be required in the future as the doom-and-gloom naysayers will be preaching their dogma louder than ever. The old big-bank system has been trying to convince you that without them the world will implode; nothing could be farther from the truth. The big banks have done little for small businesses over the past 20 years. In the mid-nineties, it seemed like the decision was made to throw small businesses under the bus; it's been downhill since then. Now, it's nearly impossible to go and get a "loan" the old-fashioned way, especially without being an established large business within a low-risk industry. Otherwise, you have to go out and find funding other ways, which can equate to giving away equity in your venture; something many entrepreneurs abhor, as that means giving up control and cow-towing to another's vision for your venture.

When was the last time you heard of an upstanding college graduate with a great business plan getting $100,000 for his new startup from a major bank? I hope you're still laughing, because you should be—as that would be a pipe dream to receive that amount of funding from today's financial institutions. If you can believe it, Americans used to actually have access that amount of funding for startups. Granted, it was mainly for the Caucasian and Asian populations, but still it was possible for some. From 1970-1998, financing a business this way was probably a feasible game plan for a fledgling upstart.

These days, forget about it even with good credit; the American politicians and big banks have given the big middle finger to small businesses and the middle class. They have said "to hell with small businesses" while trying to convince John Q. Public that small businesses don't contribute much. Sadly, nothing could be further from the truth. This country was built on the backs of small businesses and freelancers alike—lest I remind you that every big business was once a small business itself. As has been stated in many other alternative texts, corporations were not even allowed in America until the mid-1800s, as they were viewed as a dangerous power monopoly.

When you go with the flow, things assume their natural course; conversely, when the universe forces change upon you, things can get ugly. This regressive form of obstinate behavior can be an intense source of pain; yet, it seems that many people remain gluttons for punishment. As the Buddha said, "Attachment is the root of all suffering."

Salty-Dog Economics

Although the old-world economists are trying to convince us that the old economic models are indispensable, we must resist this regressive dogma. If we are to allow ourselves room to change things for the better, we must first allow change in general. Every transition has a shaky in-between period. No one can dam up the rivers of time;

so, even those incapable of change will be forced out of their comfort zones during the economic reorientation. Though there are large external changes that will be occurring due to crowdfunding and the instability of the current economic system, they merely represent external extensions of a primarily psychological shift going on within the populace. Being that most of our populace is psychologically very unstable, it would only make sense that our economy would also follow suit; hence, the true solutions lie within.

In economics, profits can't exist without losses. Learning to accept both is always advised. Becoming comfortable with the destruction inherent within nature, within economics, and within ourselves is something we all could use a lesson in. Destruction is the first step to any meaningful change; and developing a stable economy is no exception. This destructive process merely serves as a means to destroy the false things within us and within the society at large; hence, they are not to be feared.

Luckily, even this economic cloud has a silver lining— as this shift in financing economics will help bring us closer to ourselves. Even if stock markets and global currencies do go bust, there's really nothing to fear. Americans are too innovative to be broke for too long; and crowdfunding is a global phenomenon. Rich people will always exist somewhere in the world. The healthy dose of uncertainty that occurs, in the meantime, might help us to wash away the stodgy bureaucratic nature of the current fiscal claptrap. Although humankind does require stability for inner growth, the unholy amount of spiritual stagnation within our current corporate structures is abhorrent. This economic game-changer is past due in my opinion; philosophically speaking, less is more. So, the more streamlined we can make things during this fiscal retrofit, the better off we will be. These streamlining techniques will also allow us to be more in the moment, lending us more time to create meaningful changes within our personal lives as well.

Creating economic solutions that are in tune with humanity's inherent vocational potential is something that involves a lot of self-discovery: a process that scares many people, as it involves withdrawal from the outside world. It forces us to reconsider nature's role in our world. It allows us time for quiet observation; and allows us to work on breaking old patterns of behavior. Dealing with their inner psyche has never been a forte of the human race. There are many gifted alternative healers and Eastern medical practitioners who are capable of digging deep to deal with these root issues. This cathartic process can bring up some uncomfortable feelings and regrets about our past, but it's all for the best. Better to deal with your baggage now then to leave the dirty work for your children, who will be forced to either clean up your mess or repeat many of your mistakes. The fact is that until we start addressing these deeper internal problems individually, we will remain in this state of suspended development as a society. If you can't trust yourself, then who can you trust? We will be stuck in a world that is unresponsive to our needs and wholly unconcerned with our overall wellbeing.

"Love all, trust a few, do wrong to none."
—William Shakespeare, *All's Well That Ends Well*

Who's the Boss?

Utilizing this new, more fluid, economic process, we will be able to easily make changes—as they won't be dammed up by bureaucracies of the past. These internal changes will, in turn, lead to momentous business achievements and great works of art to be enjoyed by all. The fixed and rigid energies of the economic past have made a lot of people rich; but, overall, I feel they have mostly served to recreate the master/slave dynamic within our communities. The current work model generally serves to recreate the dysfunctional home life that permeates the lives of many American children. As they say, "Bullshit rolls downhill." The father gets a verbal berating from the boss and, in turn, is liable to take out that aggression on his wife and kids. Without significant time spent in nature, in meditation, or in some form of cathartic or physical creative pursuit, this emotional imbalance has no choice but to be repressed—or to come out in some unhealthy way. Our current system creates a cycle where jobs merely serve as a template to perpetuate our old emotional patterns. As a society, we should entertain the idea of healing our overall sense of self-respect. This would go a long way in easing hierarchical quarrels.

Hopefully, businesses of the future will allow us to turn off this traumatic feedback loop and get back to basics: making friends of our inner selves, our families, and our communities. Although people are hiding behind technology for now, I feel that this, too, will wane. The endless curiosity of the younger generations will push them past these outmoded technologies quicker than expected. Pretty soon, video games will be passé and new adventures for the human soul will need to be experienced. As people realize the long-term effects that these technologies are having on their children and on themselves, they might begin to fall out of favor. I myself was a total video-game addict; it's one of the biggest changes I would make if I were to have children someday. I had some fun while playing them, but I now realize the psychotic emotional state I was in and how deep the gaming addiction truly goes. It creates little virtual crackheads. Anyone who thinks differently has never had a true video-game addiction. Obviously, this addiction is compounded by not wanting to face the undesirable reality many children experience. Again, there's no one-size-fit-all way to do it, but I posit that the youth of tomorrow will be much more sane and well-adjusted spending more time in nature and less time in the virtual programming grid.

In my eyes, crowdfunding represents a larger philosophical change; a change that will allow us to take a more active part in overall societal development. In times past, the serfdom of humanity was forced to accept reality as it was, reporting in to the local feudal lord for the assignments and living off the land to eke out a meager existence. Although we have almost unlimited technological capacity, people are still living out the same types of feudal lifestyles. Reporting in to the local overlord in an attempt to take home a check, and then sitting down on the old couch to drink a beer: sound familiar? As many smarter men than me have lain out, humanity's thirst for monopolies stems from an inherent fear of change. It is common within most of the sociopathic and narcissistic individuals within society to gravitate toward positions of authority, as this satiates their temporary ego needs. Who is more powerful in the land than the king-makers of currency control?

Sadly, this bank battle is nothing new. This has been an ongoing war dating back to prehistory. In fact, for hundreds of years the practice of Usury (the practice of lending money at interest) was banned by the Catholic Church, as it was seen as a way to enslave the populace. It is only in modern times that we have totally lost respect for the monumental economic powers that the big banks have created. As it stands now, we are stuck dealing with the devil—foolishly allowing our money to control us. Instead, our currency could be empowering us to achieve nobler tasks; tasks that could embolden the human spirit.

Bad News for the Dollar

Within the current financial climate, the mega-banks have created a highly volatile system that is bound to collapse sooner than later. The vast amount of secrecy surrounding these large financial institutions that govern the world's economy should raise some concern. Bare minimum, we will be looking at a large restructuring of the stock market; and insolvency in some of the major banks. At which point, we may face bank runs and other capital restrictions to slow down the hyperinflation. This pretty much equates to a stressful scenario for most Americans, especially for those who are not highly liquid at the time. There will probably also is a need for some decentralized alternative currency to shore up the dollar.

Long story short, having all of your money tied up in the stock market, or other non-tangible assets, could lead to large losses for many people. This is a point that has been belabored by many alternative/libertarian/conservative economists. If you want to investigate this further, I would recommend the book "Rule By Secrecy" by Jim Marrs. Or to explore the roots of the Fed problem, you can also read "The Creature from Jekyll Island" by G. Edward Griffon. The real Gordian knot lies in the derivatives market, as it seems they cannot put the genie back in the bottle in that regard. Couple that with the endless printing of money by the Federal Reserve and you have one hell of an economic Molotov cocktail.

Again, this is not a book on fiscal strategy and I am not an economist. But, I have done enough research on these subjects to consider myself highly informed. Therefore, I feel the need to give fair warning to other fledgling entrepreneurs out there of the pending bank drama. A ploy I feel that is meant to keep people living in inherent fear and uncertainty so they have no time to start working on higher spiritual pursuits. This information actually helped a lot of my friends make a pretty penny on the gold market along with my grandma. Love you, Grammy Marilyn! Commodities have been going up due to inflation and should continue to retain their value, especially in comparison to our inflated fiat currency system. Although the Euro is gold-backed, it still has lots of problems due to the instability of the smaller economies that comprise its membership. So, it doesn't really represent a great alternative. Spain, Greece, and other socialist nations make long-term fiscal stability within the Eurozone a long shot at best.

It would seem to me that the only thing keeping the dollar afloat is the threat of force. Dominant empires have always been able to force their currencies upon other nations as a means for economic control. If the dollar makes it another decade without a major fiscal restructuring, I would be supremely surprised. The numbers just don't add up. But this is actually good news for small business, as it denotes a possible resurgence of the middle class.

It is also important to remember that these boom-and-bust cycles are historically recurring and always exist due to power monopolies. In Eastern thought, money is akin to yin energy or water. Basically, the thinking behind money is that there is nothing wrong when money is in motion. Just like a great river, when in motion the water remains fresh and pure; but when the river stops flowing, the water stagnates and becomes toxic—giving life to every form of pestilence. The same is true with money: when it sits one place too long without being put into use, it breeds evil. To me, this philosophy simply explains many of the problems of our world. When power builds up in a small percentage of the population, bad things ensue. Somehow, sociopathic people always rise to the top of power monopolies. Perhaps it's because they are supremely good at manipulation; and the average citizen just seems to lack sufficient subconscious discernment to see through their deception. This is why freedom is so difficult to ensure. Railing against the system in the conventional sense is a waste of energy, as darkness in this dimension is just a fact of life. You can spend your whole life dedicated to political reform, or restructuring society in some way, but that only represents the surface-level problem. If you really want to combat the evil, you must work on healing it from the inside out! Honestly, we can't take this whole phenomenon of evil personally. Obviously, this does not mean we should condone immorality in the world, but we must realize that evil also serves important functions in the universe. If it weren't for evil, how would good people be able to truly test their skills? The evils in society allow us to sharpen our wits, test our mettle, and they keep us prepared for any moral weaknesses that may arise within. In the *Tao Te Ching*, Lao Tzu states: "What is a bad man, but a good man's teacher?" I find this perspective to be invaluable.

I would never knowingly support evil people, but I also don't let the dark yin forces in the universe disempower my motivation or vision. We must realize that, in time, everything changes and that no evil is eternal. It's hard to say what a perfect government would look like. It has never existed to my knowledge. Hell, who wouldn't love to be free from all bureaucracy while living in a society full of people capable of competent self-governance; yet, I will leave the utopian panaceas for my daydreams, as no such scenario will be happening any time soon. Evil never goes down without a fight, which is why a philosophy of pure pacifism is so dangerous. Perhaps humans were not meant to live in huddled masses by the millions. Who knows? All I know is that government is always to be watched in the manner you would watch a five-year-old with a lighter in a room full of fireworks. In government, too many things can go wrong not to be eternally vigilant.

Back to the Future

A good pool of knowledge to draw upon in this realm is history. In Eastern culture, people generally never fully "retire," as they know when you disregard the generations of the past, you are doomed to repeat their mistakes. In those cultures, older people usually remain helpful in some capacity to their families or for the community at-large. Only in America's infinite wisdom have we decided to cast off this valuable section of the populace and label them as purposeless "takers." When America starts honoring and integrating the elders among us, then you will know that we are back on the right track. Think of it this way: when you want advice on the music industry, are you going to ask Willie Nelson or Justin Bieber? Case and point, one of them is a long-term sustainable force in the world, the other is a flash in the pan. America is so busy worshipping youth, that they have forgotten that it's a limited resource in life.

The wisdom older generations represent is priceless, especially in regards to fixing economic policy and learning how to recreate a strong family unit within America. Understanding these two topics will be imperative if we want to create a more balanced future. Generally speaking, true vocationalists never allow themselves to become bored enough to "retire." For as long as there is breath in your lungs, there will always be a new challenge to conquer and a new level of spiritual elevation to reach within yourself.

Granted, I understand why people do retire. After years of being brow-beaten and used like an old mule, it's no wonder many old people are too tired to keep going. Even though it is commonly thought of as the final career destination within society, I don't think this the case. We must re-learn how to fall in love with our vocational life so our goal isn't to stop working and sit on our duff. This updated vocational outlook is imperative if we are ever going to permanently change the economic paradigm for the better.

Ch. 4

The little crowd-funder that could!

In the near future, radical shifts in market diversity will take place as investors can now make money by funding startups and becoming shareholders at the inception of crowd-funded companies. As the traditional markets struggle to maintain consumer confidence in the next decade, something else will inevitably arise in their wake. There is just too much chicanery happening within the derivatives market for our current system to hold water in perpetuity. The stock market is just too rife with corruption, theft, and laziness to be trusted. Anyone who has all their eggs in that basket is in for a rude awakening in my opinion. Obviously, for security's sake, tangible investments are always the most secure. Yet, I would venture a guess that crowdfunding will invent a new way to hold ownership shares as well.

Imagine being able to own a meaningful stake in a small company for thousands less than the traditional buy-in price would be as a traditional venture capitalist. Crowdfunding can take your micro-loan and turn it into a gold factory if you play your cards right. If this unrestricted idea-growth mechanism does not precipitate a great investment boom, I don't know what would.

START-UP FEVER

Governmental and banking interests will eventually want to tax this system; but, if it arises organically, I don't know what they can really do about it. Regulating smaller "crowdfunding markets" out of existence might work to an extent; but if people got desperate enough, the whole system could just go underground. I think it's quite possible that this could happen if the big banks lose enough market-share due to this phenomenon. Think of the online poker sites that have been able to stay afloat even with massive regulation coming into play. Or think of downloading via torrent/file-sharing sites; that, obviously, has not gone away. Eventually, the industry has had to start embracing these facts of life, whether they like it or not. The same will be true with crowdfunding, where the genie cannot be put back in the bottle. We should remain open to the fact that the stock market for crowdfunding may have to go partially underground until regulators figure out that micro-banking is an unstoppable idea.

Crowdfunding will give the Average Joe on the street an ability to participate in penny stocks in a meaningful way—an activity that would, seemingly, be a waste of time in today's market. Like anything else, this new economic landscape won't come without a laundry list of startup problems—such as hacking, owner accountability, secure ownership transfers, false financials, etc. But, if we create tangible physical shares, then we might avoid many of these problems. Shareholders would be protected by a new standard in physical share ownership, which would prevent a lot of the market manipulation that is currently happening; and no one would be in a position to complain.

Whether these consumer exchanges will exist primarily online, or in smaller state-to-state versions, is hard to tell.

But, you can be sure that a good amount of decentralization will be a part of the process. I feel that the decline of our current economic system represents an amazing opportunity for human civilization, as it will force people once again to be active participants in their own economic destiny. Without perpetual streams of mailbox money coming in, people will be forced to once again leave their bubble world and start to actively create value over the entirety of their lives. Government welfare always creates psychological dependency amongst the populace (it's impossible for it not to) that is detrimental to spiritual individuation. It also creates a fear mentality around money: when the government is paying you, it must feel like there's never enough to go around. Granted, government can be useful for some things; but when it actively seeks to create economic dependency amongst the populace, economic growth goes into an absolute tailspin. Without being forced into reality by having to go out and get a job, many people will choose to take the easy way out and choose not to work. I can proudly say that despite my numerous stints of unemployment, I have never relegated myself to such a codependent measure. Sure, I have borrowed money, but I have never felt right about declaring myself a *de facto* ward of the state. Sadly, work is a fact of life; and without work and physical exertion, physical and spiritual decline takes place rapidly. Put succinctly: if you're not living, you're dying.

As I previously stated, decentralizing the mega-financing systems will allow for a lot more transparency, in my view. That way, these Bernie-Madoff-types can't go unnoticed for twenty years. Some trade secrecy is required within the corporate sphere. But if you are a major stakeholder in a company, you should be privy to the major financial dealings and advancements, etc. As has come out in mainstream media recently, corporate espionage has become a very prominent tactic in many larger organizations; but within the small business community, it's exceedingly rare. Generally speaking, no one is going to try and steal trade secrets unless there are millions at stake. Small businesses, generally, don't deal in the kind of revenue necessary to warrant that kind of attention. If we think of it again as a type of warfare: smaller armies have smaller battles, larger armies have larger battles.

But during an economic renaissance, we must not leave any new ideas at the door. Below, I have outlined what I feel are many of the possible alternatives with the pros and cons of each. I sincerely want to create an open debate about a future restructuring amongst the business community. This way, when it comes about everyone is a bit more prepared and able to deal with the situation maturely and assertively.

At the end of the day, everyone will be better off with more community-based economies. This is why I love crowdfunding. Though the stock market represents a cooperative phenomenon to some extent, it doesn't have the decentralized organic feel that crowdfunding has. Crowdfunding will represent something totally unique, especially when you consider the alternative currency dimensions that it produces as well. It has the potential to create hundreds of mini stock markets; and to produce continuous long-term financing as well. Eventually, startups will also be able to access second- and third-round funding via crowdfunding on the internet as well. This is only the beginning, so let's get going while the going is good!

Innovation Economies

Inevitably, during a total economic reorientation people will try their hand at a number of things in order to get things moving back in the right direction. I say try everything as there is nothing new under the sun anyhow! Variations and differentiations are the spice of life. Creativity is what keeps people lively and on their toes.

This is the type of idiosyncratic economic experimentation that can catch the bureaucrats with their pants down—as a system based on fixity can never catch up to an entrepreneurial mind which is in perpetual movement. Here's a novel idea: how about creating a system where people work together without obscene amounts of bureaucrats and lawyers taking a cut for pushing paperwork? Okay, maybe I'm in fantasyland, but I don't think anyone likes the excessive mountains of paperwork that are currently part of day-to-day mega-corporations. I say we all pick up a shovel, dig a ditch, throw some paperwork in, set it ablaze, and repeat. We shouldn't burn books; we should burn paperwork!

The simplest solutions are usually the best; so, with that in mind, let's try to kick some ass to help again restore America's innovative economic legacy. If the world is going to require some form of structure to maintain social sanity, let's at least create a structure that we can live with.

During an economic debacle, people will also try their hand at a co-op style of business. While I am a believer in the theory behind this kind of model, I think that it has too many drawbacks to be feasible for long-term usage. First and foremost, there is the problem with boundaries. If businesses can't have firm emotional boundaries, it's hard to say exactly who owes whom for what; solid payment structures are a good thing to prevent hostilities on all sides. It also creates a much more professional environment, where focus can be kept on the current task. In my experience, this communitarian structure borrows too much from the communist model, lacks sufficient incentive to produce, effectively creating an atmosphere where moochers can flourish. Co-ops for farming and certain industries are very handy, but I think you will have a hard time convincing more complex businesses of the Amish way of life. P.S.: the Amish produce the best milk ever!

I do feel that commune-style cafeterias would be very handy if they were using farm-fresh organic ingredients. You could have a group of 40-100 people pitch in to rent out a space and hire some cooks to prepare fresh food every evening if the working professionals are too busy to cook for themselves. It just makes sense in a world that has had the family unit broken into pieces; some healthy external cooking would do wonders for the American working spirit. If I could pay $50-70 a week and get two square organic meals a day, I would be doing backflips.

There is a serious communist bent to many alternative economic models, so they don't hold much water in complex economies over the long term; yet, they are very useful for short-term solutions in many cases. Getting to know your local neighbors and working together becomes key—slowly reinstating trust as the norm of our species. If we maintain the current system of always trying to one-up our neighbor for the ego's sake, our hearts can never truly rest. Materialism is an endless quest. As Buddha said, "Give a man a mountain of gold and he will ask for a second." Besides basic food and shelter, what do humans really require to survive and thrive, existentially speaking? Love? Money? Friendship? Health? At times in life, we may be deprived of one or all of these things; so, I feel that part of our larger quest is to learn how to be content within ourselves. Even life itself—a precious and fragile thing—is transient. When we are able to be comfortable with our own death, and view death as an ally, we can start living a life free of regrets. In the words of Lao Tzu, "If I fear not death, what can harm me?"

Riding the App wave…

Mobile apps have more than taken on a life of their own; and entire large-scale businesses are now being built around the mobile phenomenon. Companies such as Waze, Lyft, and Uber are really taking the marketplace by storm—giving conventional business models a run for their money. Why shouldn't crowdfunding also bring these new apps into existence? Appfunder.com is trying to do that in its own way: they are providing an independent analysis of new phone app marketability and trying to open up avenues for new apps to gain traction in the online world! There's no limit to the app ideas that could be funded through these new modalities. Everybody loves a handy app. Pretty soon, they will have apps that reintegrate humans back into the real (non-digital) world!

START-UP FEVER

At the rate our society is headed, being outdoors will soon be a groundbreaking idea.

This is especially true when you walk into a twenty-something's joint and everyone is staring at their little glowing screens! Apps will eventually be plugged into every area of human life. We will soon be even more inundated by this post-digital phenomenon. Some inventive people will come along and find a way to integrate this technology in an emotionally healthy way. No manmade technology can supersede the inter-dimensional majesty that is present within nature. But if there's a buck to be made, inevitably someone will give it a try—whether it's a benevolent idea or not. Again, you can't have the good without the bad, so we must maintain a state of constant moral vigilance. Other ideas inside the mobile phone realm include:

- ✓ Build new types of cell phones which run fully encrypted all the time

- ✓ Integrate the 3-D printer with the mobile phenomenon in schools so children can experiment with making high-end production and communication more efficient.

- ✓ Create a mobile stock market that supports only small business. This is something that could definitely cause a mobile penny-stock boom. Giving valuable investment dollars to companies and allowing small-time investors legitimate returns on their money.

- ✓ Deliver groceries with mobile services.

- ✓ Create mobile shopping lists and pre-orders for local farmer's markets. There's a lot we can do to make things more local; thereby, eliminating costly transport and excess taxation. I feel like the world will can continue its technological ascent if it's done in a thoughtful manner.

Turning Pitchforks into Swords….

The way I see it, crowdfunding will instigate a wave of asymmetrical warfare within the business world; and there's nothing big business can do about it. I'm sure the more astute financial forecasters out there are aware of this, but they are probably unable to come forward with their findings for one reason or another. I have heard Cathryn Austin Fitts and many other alternative researchers speak about this trend, but it's going to take more active participation from the larger business leaders in the world to be successful. Change is a slow process, so I always advise immense patience. It took thousands of years to create problems. So, it may also take considerable time to fix them. But with everyone doing a small part, our lives can again become more sane, happy, and peaceful than at any previous point in history.

Even though crowdfunding cuts down on the overall interference from the banks into fiscal affairs, it by no means cuts them out completely. Banks still control the vast majority of cash flow; and until competing currencies or alternative modes of exchange are developed, there will be little that can be done to change the dependence on these immense fiscal institutions. In the words of Morpheus in *The Matrix*, "They are guarding all the doors. They are holding all the keys, which means that, sooner or later, someone is going to have to fight them."

START-UP FEVER

As fate would have it, it seems that crowdfunding is one of the main models that will help to put a few of these mega-corporations back in check—or checkmate. There is a saying in the Dao, "Take the good, and leave the bad." It's a saying that seems simple, but is ultimately profound. If we can take what worked well from the old system and leave the rest for the vultures to fight over, we will be well on our way to a much brighter fiscal outlook.

Historically wars have almost always been fought for money and power. Everyone involved in business must struggle against something. Doctors combat illness. Janitors combat dirt and grime. Chefs combat hunger, and so on. As Michael Tsarion has so succinctly pointed out: what is the hidden meaning behind putting on a suit and tie? It represents nothing more than a modern-day suit of armor. Where else did you think that term would come from? After you put on your monkey suit, you report to the local modern-day commander: your boss. Many people work in modern phallic towers known as skyscrapers. In olden times, the taller the building was, the more power it was thought to be able to conjure; a theory which still must hold some water in wealthy circles, as powerful banks are usually found in these downtown mega-towers.

We can begin to see that although we have a new window dressing, psychologically not much has changed. We are still putting on our armor, shutting down our emotions, and driving into our little armored fortresses to do battle with the larger economic world. Many of these poor souls have seen fit to declare war on the modern Middle American who is standing clueless in the crossfire. It's about time we sharpened our economic wits and started firing back, theologically, instead of being at the whim of the machine. If we cannot cultivate an individualistic form of economic self-defense, we will always be dependent upon someone outside ourselves for our own economic stability—an idea that I, for one, am not comfortable with in the least. I was a corporate lackey for too many years to be okay with being an indentured servant to the machine for the rest of my days.

According to Sun Tzu, "To win a battle, you must first understand yourself. Secondly, you must understand your enemy." If you don't understand yourself or your opponent, how can you even begin to understand the nature of the conflict? Economic warfare has existed since the beginning days of monarchical and patriarchal societies. We must understand that vast concentrations of wealth are nothing new. In essence, we must individually redefine our relationship to money and transmute any lingering spiritual hang-ups we have about creating it—or using it properly. In the tarot, the five of pentacles represents the concept of maturing fiscally. It represents the phase where the adept learns the hard way how to give to himself in a deep and meaningful way. This is accomplished by not squandering money needlessly on the pseudo-marketing dreams that the world economy has sold us. Why are we required to purchase other people's dreams, just to feel good about living in our own—and at a premium no less? If we don't grab the helm of this directionless economic ship, we will soon be sailing into some dark water, which could be more dangerous than we know. We were gifted with spirituality for a reason: so that we may be able to reach the higher intelligence in the universe to help us solve even the most difficult worldly problems. Deep down, we all intrinsically know what to do. If only we had to patience and courage to find those solutions within ourselves.

With regards to our current economic battles, I say: "To arms!" Start building your psychological defenses against the impending fiscal attack. Start with yourself: ask yourself why you feel the need to be fiscally dependent upon someone else for your own material welfare. Ask yourself how you see a better economic system working. Ask yourself what type of people you would like to work with in the future. Ask yourself what business you would crowd-fund for yourself if money were no object. Ask yourself how that business would create value for your loved ones and the community at-large. Ask yourself whether the city or town you live in is capable of supporting your dream or if you need to move to make your dreams into realities. After you have let go of all of the dreams that other people have sold you, you can begin to conceptualize a unique vision for your own life. When you have reached that point where you have a totally idiosyncratic vision for your life, then you are about ready to begin!

Getting a grip on your own emotional and spiritual life is the number-one priority. Once you start gaining a good amount of internal momentum in your own spiritual development, then you will naturally start feeling prepared to put some of these newfound principles to work out into the larger world. Giving your economic skill set freely to the outside world is one of the most rewarding things you will ever have the opportunity to do. A vocation in action is a very powerful thing, as one vocationally empowered man or woman is capable of curing countless imbalances and injustices in the world. These small-scale economic and community reforms can be tackled in numerous ways.

A few ideas include:

- ✓ Work together to fund community businesses.

- ✓ Build your own local internet (intranet) to host community transactions and act as a server for local websites.

- ✓ Help build a framework for sustainable community co-op farming.

- ✓ Increase your knowledge of local flora and fauna.

- ✓ Develop Micro FM radio stations for beneficial informational programming.

- ✓ Build your own 3D community printing facility and rent it out to local designers at an hourly rate. It would be a Kinko's for 3D programmers.

- ✓ Hold community classes on innovation and study local pioneers, gleaning what you can from their methods.

- ✓ Build positive educational video games that are still interesting and engaging, but not psychologically warping to the youth.

- ✓ Start clubs and entrepreneurship at the local high schools to start motivating kids with new ideas; also a great recruiting technique.

- ✓ Reconnect with the natural cycles of time through recreating a new type of calendar that refines our conception of time and how it should be used.

- ✓ Avoid the urge to celebrate every weekend as if you had just won an Olympic medal.

START-UP FEVER

- ✓ Consult the local elders for their input on community developments.

- ✓ Help implement alternative forms of drug rehabilitation within the community.

- ✓ Coordinate local cultural enrichment activities.

- ✓ Help your neighbors identify their own strengths with which to start their own ventures.

- ✓ Create community service pools for skilled labor.

- ✓ Develop your own local currency.

- ✓ Consider available local resources and work within the framework of nature.

- ✓ Use some small-scale teamwork to help improve plant and animal life in the area

This process involves finding yourself first and worrying about your true friends and family second. If your friends and family are not supportive of you, then that generally means they are scared to find themselves; and you should never allow other people's fear to hold you back. When it comes to naysayers, we must remember the bigger they come, the harder they fall. If we can keep the economics simple, then businesses will grow naturally according to market demand. And less market manipulation will be possible.

Some of these solutions may seem extreme and, perhaps, they are. I want to make sure you realize that the economy can be successfully run in a thousand different ways. We are totally capable of reinventing a system that doesn't bond us to debt-slavery, high taxation, mass incarceration, and mass drug addiction as our current system does. A perfect example is the Amish community. They live totally off the grid and don't seem to be suicidal or strung out on drugs of any kind. They seem to be getting along just fine and have plenty of cash to go around. Even if everything within modern society falls apart, I can guarantee that the Amish way of life will be alive and kicking. Granted, I understand this is an offbeat way of life, but it still serves to show that societies can function thousands of ways.

No matter how you slice it, entrepreneurship will always be a battle. The game just changes as you go up the ladder. At the low level, it's your family and friends who can doubt you and make you second guess yourself. They might turn against you if they feel that you will end up failing or if your personal change threatens the existing relationship between you. Sometimes, your business will just make people insecure and make them feel like they aren't good enough since they haven't started something themselves. Jealousy is to be expected, but envy is the nasty bugger you have to watch out for. At the median level, your challenges will be coming from other startups, intimate relationships, accounting, and finding financing among other things. At the larger level, you will run up against other competitive businesses, the government, espionage, employees, and disruptive technologies that can hurt your business model.

No matter where you are, there will always be a challenge. Our duty is to embrace the challenges of life and learn to enjoy the opportunities. Entrepreneurial minds don't see problems, they create solutions. To be a solution-oriented individual is to be flexible; to be flexible allows you not to break. Trust me: any form of entrepreneurial endeavor will be sure to test your patience—and your sanity.

START-UP FEVER

Crowdfunding will, for all intents and purposes, become a major vehicle for the lower- and middle-class working Americans to regain their self-respect. We need to ride this change as far and as fast as it will take us. This is a fiscal weapon that is long overdue. Thank God someone had the bright idea to cut out the banks from small business affairs—banks who have promised security and delivered little more than a stalled economy. Luckily, crowdfunding and the elbow grease of moral virtuous people will always be there to pick up the pieces.

Although success is possible no matter what the circumstances, sometimes things come along that make victory much more likely. Freedom became more likely with the advent of the printing press as information became more difficult to control. During our age, the internet has brought about another type of revolution— one that is being taken full advantage of by the pioneers of the world. The internet is an intellectual reformer not to be underestimated. If we can get past the smut and the timewasters, we can actually get our society back on track faster than ever. The inception of America also brought with it the adoption of free-market economics, which bred a successful and upwardly mobile society. Anyone who was willing to work hard had a chance to succeed. This is still true to an extent, even though there is now enough red tape to strangle the Kool-Aid guy. All red tape aside, the bottom line remains that freedom is the true driver of economic growth. Less freedom, less growth; more taxes, less growth. It's as simple as that. Paradoxically, when you abuse freedom, you enslave yourself. So, we can begin to see how this cycle perpetuates itself.

The people who founded this great nation were not afraid to die for their economic freedom. For us to regain our autonomy, we must also be prepared to adopt a modern sense of fearlessness. For a life lived in fear is a life half lived. This is why we must first purify and rectify the intentions of our economic purpose. If we intend to go forward with external weapons, we will be fighting with obsolete tools. We cannot win a spiritual war with physical weapons. Nor can we defeat our enemies when we do battle within a system that we did not create; so, the American Dream must create a new vision for the economic system that negates the usefulness of the old one. We must go forward with internally forged economic weapons so we can be victorious in the epoch ahead. It's a battle to be fought with ideas, not bullets; and even though it is always an option, it is less favored these days, as it destroys valuable infrastructure and is bad for political careers.

The internet represents the new battleground, as it is merely an extension of the super-conscious—or perhaps the subconscious depending on how you look at it. Nothing on this earth can truly imitate the workings of the Dao or god; but at the very least, the internet is a representation of the inner workings of the human mind. Using the internet as a barometer to gauge the health of the collective human psyche, I would say the findings are sketchy at best. It is clear that humans are waist high in escapist internet quicksand, trying just about anything to avoid taking a hard look at their lives. It's time to become an economic doctor in your own capacity. We can help restore balance to the world through starting businesses that promote sanity, community, morality, and human dignity—not by starting businesses that destroy the fabric of our society.

Stockbrokers go to war with computers every day, fighting the ones and zeros of the digital algorithms that now control the markets. Derivatives are governed by these inane systems of control. Man is already at war against machines, as these algorithms are more in control of our markets than physical people are—as has been referenced in expose films such as *Margin Call*. We might as well have Frankenstein himself pulling the levers of Wall Street.

If we take this warfare model as an assumption, it's easy to see how this newfound liquidity within the small business market will allow consumers to more effectively vote with their dollars and send outdated models to a shallow grave. This is a phenomenon we are already witnessing within the organic food community, where smaller farmers and respectable growing practices are quickly gaining ground on the GMO conglomerates that have dominated the market for decades. If the battle against Monsanto does not represent warfare, I don't know what does. Hundreds of thousands of Americans have taken up arms against these parasitical buggers. If one thing can be deciphered from this battle, it's that whatever you do, don't mess with America's food. Because we like to eat!

Our hope should be that this phenomenon follows into all other sectors of the economy, effectively giving the average citizen a more-informed platform to make purchasing decisions by accessing the transparency offered by many smaller businesses—transparency that will also be forced by the new crowdfunding mechanisms that are requiring many businesses to maintain open books.

For those who fear nothing but the worst can happen, I say that we have never been at such a benevolent information advantage in all of human history. You can learn virtually anything you want in an afternoon on YouTube. So, with every piece on information available to us, I honestly do not see how our economy can be lost!

Ch. 5
The Boom without the Boom!

L uckily for the little guy, crowdfunding, cross-promotional platforms, and other micro-funding mechanisms are starting to level the economic playing field quite a bit—allowing many young fledgling entrepreneurs to flourish in an otherwise slow-moving investment pool. Granted, the average American's dispensable income may be at a thirty-year low. But as they say, "if it isn't one thing it's another." No economic decline lasts forever. And if you can become profitable during the lean times, just imagine how you might prosper during a true economic boom—a boom which we are destined to see again within our lifetimes. As the Buddhist saying goes, "winter always turns to spring." So, it's only a matter of getting through a deconstructive phase of our current economic system before the boom cycle happens once again. This may sound harsh, but the market as it stands is ultimately unsustainable, as no country can finance their way out of hard work forever. It should also be noted that economies based on warfare also break down over time, as no actual wealth is actually created during war; it's merely an illusion of short-term profitability that masks the long-term losses.

Losses rooted in obsolete equipment creation, health care costs, and the destruction of countrywide morale. Entrepreneurs must plan accordingly and make use of the changing tides.

Even in the event of an economic restructuring, the crowdfunding method presents a perfect vehicle with which to renovate models based on the new digital capitalism. It seems obvious to me that a "national free market" is very improbable within the near future, but that does not mean we can't acquire some freedom on the local level by using these models. When it comes to theorizing about boom-and-bust cycles it is always important to focus foremost on the personal development of the populace—as personal development is one of the prime drivers behind real wealth within society. Places in which people possess self-respect and a healthy work ethic usually have much more sustainable economic systems. Think about it: wouldn't it make sense that a happy and emotionally self-assured workforce would be more productive than one that is dejected and soul-less? Through gross over-taxation, the American people have largely been robbed of the rewards of their labor and instead have been handed community works projects.

At the end of the day, someone with inherent self-worth will be able to make a living no matter what external economic events may crop up. The key to thriving during any major change is not to live in fear. Whatever happens, happens. Let the chips fall where they may. But always do your best! Destruction is a perfectly natural part of life and should be accepted as such.

With crowdfunding quickly becoming one of the main financing engines in our economic sphere, a more healthy economic revolution is not far off—helping to bring American small businesses back to life. As evidenced by the massive success of sites such as Kickstarter and Indiegogo, the beginning stage of this sizeable crowdfunding boom has already begun. It is a mystery to me why the business community hasn't made a bigger deal about these recent upstart wonders. Perhaps they are as scared of change as anyone.

I would venture a guess and say that the mass media's relative silence on these issues is due to other looming political and economic concerns. Couple that with the fact that it seems like the corporate media, in general, focuses on doom and gloom, I guess it's hard for most people to hear good economic news when they can't yet see it outside their window—as this is largely a revolution still percolating in entrepreneurial minds all across America.

Academia is certainly not offering any legitimate solutions to our fiscal predicaments; instead, we just receive more Stone-Age economic dribble. If there's one thing I know, it's that the people actively creating the problems in our world can't be trusted to create solid solutions to our issues! This is why I am urging the general populace to look to children, nature, alternative economists, and trailblazers for true economic solutions; the world only moves forward and we can't live our lives in reverse, hoping for the economic "good times" to come back. If by economic "good times" we are referencing the drug-induced psychopathic frenzy that has destroyed families nationwide over the past 50 years, we can only pray those "good times" never come back!

Economic analysts seem to be worried about the ensconced corporations who are going out of business by the dozen. They also seem to be doing a good job at freaking out a vast majority of our nation's elderly in the process. Although on the surface things may seem bleak, I can assure you that these economic cycles amount to little more than nature taking its natural course. Despite man's best efforts, he has not been able to completely extricate nature from his modern corporate world. Glass is still made out of finely ground rocks, houses are still framed with the wood from trees, and skyscrapers are still made from metal within the earth. No matter how modern man may try to be, nature is still irrevocably part of our society; therefore, its natural cycles are as applicable as ever. It doesn't matter how many gadgets you own: you will never be able to avoid the wind or live without water—nor would you be able to take a step without treading upon the earth. Everything faces death in some form or another, even businesses. I know that these mega-conglomerates represent jobs for many people, but they can also represent a society that is desperately clinging to the past.

Taxes? That's so 1775....

As it stands now, taxes in America are at an all-time high, something that any economist worth their salt will tell you is a bad sign for growth. Large companies are trying desperately to turn a profit while governmental officials don't seem to understand that many of these 100-year-old companies operate on very low margins. Having a 5%-15% profit margin does not leave much room for error. So, with taxes going up across the board, bigger corporations have no choice but to dodge taxes in many cases. Obviously, there are lots of exceptions; but, long story short, everyone is in business to make money and when the system is rigged against you, it can be very hard to turn a profit as a modern small business. As Ayn Rand predicted, if politics keeps going in this direction, only the largest and most corrupt enterprises will remain—using all of their wealth and all of the politically based tax exemptions to leech off of the public.

> "The only power any government has is the power to crack down on criminals. Well, when there aren't enough criminals, one makes them. One declares so many things to be a crime that it becomes impossible for men to live without breaking laws."
> —Ayn Rand, "Atlas Shrugged"

Think about it; if you had a hundred-year-old business that would be forced into bankruptcy if you did not hire teams of lobbyists to change tax laws so you could stay in existence, then you may think about hiring some lobbyists. It's as simple as that. Evil or not, many times the business world confronts humanity with many morally grey areas—where it's hard to say what the virtuous resolution is. At high levels of business, many people don't play fair. Again, I don't have all the answers, I just want to paint a fair picture of what's happening, to create awareness and open a dialogue on issues. At this point in America, we are trying to save the last bastion of small businesses that have been able to weather the continuous assault via taxation and regulation, alike.

Besides big tax hikes, these big corporations are going out of business because they can't morph their business models fast enough to keep up. Let's face it: brick and mortar had its heyday. In modern terms, that's one of the most difficult businesses to maintain; anything with lots of overhead and high margins is a risky play in today's economic climate. When you bet big, you can also lose big. This is where the "Generation Y" crowd has come in to institute some old-school bootstrapping models. As a matter of necessity, I believe we will begin to see the Gen-Y crowd become more and more fiscally conservative with their startups. I hope that as the younger leaders emerge, they will begin to see the errors of the licentious business culture of the last thirty years. By taking a look around, it's not hard to find a few corporate types pissing away their spiritual impetus at the local bar. This common existential depression is something that businesses of the future must start to address. From my research, many prominent innovators usually abstain from such intoxicants, as they realize the loss of energy and vitality that is accompanied by purely pleasure-based pursuits.

Besides just the physical loss of energy, these activities can also lead to bad dreams and poor sleep, as the subconscious rebels in its attempt to regain spiritual dominion. No soul wants to get permanently attached to the ego because that represents a prison sentence condemning on to never achieving any spiritual progress. Again, in the fight for ourselves, fear remains the main enemy. If people are not plagued with the fear of a potential loss in money and job security, then they are plagued with the fear of not being able to provide for their families. But, Americans of the future need to take a good hard look at the damage caused by these morally devoid career options. Selling out our ethics and compromising with the low moral standards of the general public leaves us mentally impoverished. Only those with some form of economic morality are truly fit to lead this fiscal resurgence, so let's hope some of the cream rises to the top.

Gen-Y do you ask?

The Gen-Y tech boom has produced astounding innovations in modern technology; although, it has yet to generate the same fiscal success as the "dot com boom" did. Granted, by the time many of the Gen-Y kids were running startups, the country was already in fiscal decline. I view the Gen-Y boom as more of a revolution of ideas. It's clear that many of these new businesses are extremely inventive; yet, profit does not seem to be the overarching motive. Hell, even the likes of YouTube failed to turn a profit during its five-year mega-expansion before being acquired by Google. Is it possible that is happened because profits had taken a backseat to vision? Or was it just a dream without any forethought about monetization? Or was all of the money to be made illegally through selling users' viewing habits? Who knows? However you look at it, obviously, they did turn a profit eventually by selling out to Google—for a dump truck full of cash no less.

The problem with many of the new Gen-X tech-boom companies seems to lie in achieving profitability through legitimate means. Instead of being above board with financial struggles, many of these fledgling startups have decided to start selling personal information as a stopgap measure. This problem is rampant in the app community, where people sell personal information like hotcakes. There has to be a better way to make money than spying and mind-screwing the slower-thinking portions of society.

Websites like Facebook, SoundCloud, Pandora, and Myspace have all struggled with profitability, as they don't really produce anything other than information—which can only be sold and sliced so many ways, much to the chagrin of both business and the unwitting consumer. It seems to me that for many of these companies, the idea seems to be more important. They seem to be betting that they can monetize their business models long term by some form of unknown magic formula. I don't see this current phase as being viable long term, so we can expect a more pay-to-play model of the internet emerge in the future, when things get a bit more costly as companies are forced to pass on direct expenses to the consumer.

By virtue of necessity, the younger generations have started to create a new version of a lean, mean, startup machine. This new model, which has emerged mostly due to crowdfunding, has been engineered to combat tax hikes and prevent massive overheads. Unfortunately, the remedies can equate to exporting jobs and cutting hours and benefits; but, it's really the only way to operate under current policies in many cases. Nobody is going to start a small business that plans on losing money for five years upfront, which is how many of these wealthier startups operate. Obviously, greed will also play a part in this equation, but that is always a risk that you take when you give people freedom. It's still a hell of a lot better than expecting some external company or authority to provide for your personal welfare. So, for the time being, we are forced to chalk these newer policies up as the cost of doing business. Anyone competing on the low to mid end of the price spectrum will have problems turning a profit with all of the new taxes in place. Until major economic policy shifts, or major economic upheaval hits, we are going to just have to learn to live with it; obviously, supporting local economies whenever possible. Realistically speaking, not everything can be made locally in a global economy. At the end of the day, the best we can do is follow our inner sense of morality and try our best to do right by everyone with whom we come into contact. Cheating others is to cheat ourselves.

This upcoming psychological shift in corporate America can be witnessed through the context of the emo movement: a teenage movement where emotionalism and existential angst was brought to the forefront of pop culture. Although not showing any clear path out of the delirium, it does serve to show us what's on the mind of the global consciousness. There is also a neo-hipster minimalist style of music emerging as well. Hopefully, this trend represents a subconscious desire from the population to return to a simpler lifestyle. The beats and compositions are very basic, but at least they seem to be somewhat harmonious and calming to the soul overall—even if the lyrical stylings leave much to be desired in terms of their depth of thought.

It's not just the Emo/Neo-Hipster trends we are contending with in future psychological economic reform; we also must account for the mind control coming out of the mainstream rap and pop music worlds. In my opinion, the mainstream versions of these genres have been turning into an outlet for the worst part of our shadow natures. The lower end of these genres exhibits the worst of our collective narcissism—effectively driving the youth to worship an economic theology that seeks to enslave them. If you listen closely to the lyrics, you will find that the content mirrors corporate America: warping the American Dream into one in which the one who gets ahead is the one willing to sell their soul to get to the top. While promising the fragile youth a world full of limitless hedonism in which emotions represents a form a weakness and other people are merely pawns to be controlled. Not exactly a great message for good business developments or an evolution of the modern corporate worker. If you remember in the movie *Office Space*, Michael Bolton, one of the junior programmers at Innotech, is bumping some gangster rap in his car ride to work. Hilarious as this may be, it really is true to life in many senses, as these gangbanging role models represent a breed of imposter folk heroes to the young corporate workers—heroes who present a destructive alternative to living outside of the corporate system. Effectively serving as little more than pied pipers to lead people away from themselves.

Neo Workspace!

As these emotionally lost teens get older, there will be a leap forward in personal expressionism within the workplace. This trend can already be seen with the dispersion of the whole cube-farm phenomena—a large office of nothing but cubicles—and the movement toward a much more ascetically pleasing office environment. Many of the West Coast offices have some really amazing workspaces, especially some of the tech startups. It is interesting that they call these worksites a work "campus." Does this reflect the perpetually suspended state of the psyche—a state in which employees are forced to suspend their journey into true adulthood?

While younger people become more sensitive to their environments, we will see more and more corporations refusing to occupy the monotone buildings of the past. Hopefully, this trend will also represent a return to work environments that include nature as a central planning element. Someone has to get rid of the modern abomination that is florescent lighting. Florescent lighting presents serious long-term health hazards and is totally unnatural for the human body. Daylight is obviously optimal; but if we must be caged in, daylight-balanced lighting is much better. The serious imbalances in florescent lightings frequency spectrum can cause depression, anxiety, and drowsiness. For those interested in the studies behind these findings, I would refer you to "Light, Medicine of the Future" by Dr. John Ott, a pioneer within this field.

Among all the psychological dissociation, many of our younger brethren have become incredibly confused with identifying gender roles, especially within the more urban/metropolitan environments. What's causing this particular phenomenon—other than too much BPA in the plastic—is that men have forgotten how to be men; and women have forgotten how to be women. Leaving many young partying bohemians confused about true masculine and feminine roles in a constructive society. Hopefully, the younger generations can begin to work through these identity issues and begin detach from the collective and form a stronger sense of self—but I am not holding my breath. I am honestly as perplexed by anyone on this issue, but I know that it exists. On the whole, patriarchy has traditionally been blamed for many ills in society; although, if you look at the figures, women's liberation hasn't helped preserve domestic harmony at all. If anything, it just puts more focus on consumerist culture and less focus on the children. Again, I don't proclaim any easy answers to a new American Dream; I just know that things can't go on as is, as the kids are the ones truly paying the price for all of the moral disarray in society. Last time I checked, fifty percent of the population was still female, so we can't leave them out of the discussion of how this whole societal debacle got started.

Baby Billionaires

A very interesting point in this discussion is the age of the average billionaire is quickly dipping lower and lower. I would imagine that the average age of the world's wealthiest people is much lower than it was ten years ago. Let's hope that having more capital in the hands of the younger generations will create a more emotional, balanced, shift. It is always possible that some of the world's ultra-rich could give away their fortunes in the pursuit of building a healthier, more psychologically stable, society. Even if,, the "Julius Cesar types who abolish all debt for the poor are a rarity; the hope being that some of the younger entrepreneurial crowd could be more in touch with the sufferings of humanity than the older, more callused, crowd.

You can rest assured that even with proper funding, the development of a sure-footed sense of emotional balance and fiscal integrity won't happen overnight. In a culture of greed, it's hard to know where to invest charitable dollars as charities can usurp money just as quickly as any other company. As it stands now, the tech Nuevo-rich still seem to be stuck within the rap-video mentality. Perhaps, a new type of corporate executive will have to emerge before people start to see what a benevolent fiscal innovator can actually accomplish.

Although this newfound crowdfunding boom is promising, it will not occur without its own set of challenges. It seems like every undergrad business major you meet has a crappy app that's only sold about 20 copies on the iTunes store; but, hey, at least they are giving it a shot. Yet, when you understand the power of viral marketing, you quickly realize that with the right hook anything is possible.

It's hard to say how all of these young billionaire techies will propagate their legacies, but you can rest assured that many of these twenty-somethings constitute a different breed. Some of these young tech gurus seem to be totally hyper-focused technologically, leaving no room to lead a balanced lifestyle. This trend is disturbing when you consider the monkey-see-monkey-do aftereffects. In many corporate environments, being the dominant figure is still defined by a level of high sexual prowess and a gluttonous appetite for the nightlife. Beyond that: if you watch some sports and hit up some of the old boys' endowment functions, then you're soon to be in the "in crowd." You will be glad-handing your way to corporate success in no time.

Ch. 6

Future shock, a new upstart for a new generation

The larger your business is, the harder it is to hit the moving targets that exist in the modern world. These moving targets present opportunities for startups to succeed by playing *Johnny on the Spot*, helping to fill unique niches in the marketplace—niches that only a few Google-sized companies with more money than sense can, effectively, start overnight. This silent startup boom has come about due to the explosive emergence of low-cost marketing, cell-phone apps, new digital marketplaces, and crowdfunding. Although Groupon has effectively gone from hero to zero, the business model that they presented has changed the business landscape forever.

For those who don't know, Groupon is one of many daily deal sites that allow groups of 50-5000 people to buy a gift certificate to a business for some pre-ordained service—massages, car washes, cupcakes etc.—for a large discount (usually 50 percent of more). This, in turn, allows the business to generate lump sums of money (paid out by Groupon) to fulfill these orders; and guarantees them new customers to frequent their location—effectively creating an instant clientele for any new business. In theory, if the product or service that is offered from the promotion is exemplary, then word of mouth will build enough client momentum to keep the business afloat—allowing the business an opportunity to give it "the old college try" at turning a profit.

The underlying economic issue here is that daily deal sites are redefining the metrics of volume, especially for small- and medium-sized businesses. I truly believe that if it was not for Groupon, then the whole concept of crowdfunding might not exist. Since the passage of the recent crowdfunding bill (the JOBS act), no longer will accredited investors (those with a net worth of one million dollars or more) be the only ones invited to the startup party. Due to the passage of the JOBS Act, pretty much anyone will be able to have a say in which companies are able to make it to market. Crowdfunding sites such as www.crowdfunding.com have paved the way for Everyday Joes to become legitimate angel investors, instead of just stockholders; allowing room for riskier, and more inventive, business models to emerge. Groupon was one of the first to emerge as a leader utilizing these new business models.

Daily Deals Sites, Friend or Foe?

Many people within the startup community have heard the Daily Deal startup success stories—juxtaposed with a few horror stories as well. The fact is that Daily Deals will always represent a good model for cross-promotional opportunities in the marketplace—as there is always some other company out there who you can effectively link up with to increase your business. Even though Groupon and the like are effectively defunct due to poor planning and fiscal mismanagement, it doesn't mean what they achieved is not radically important. Obviously, your business model needs to be compelling and your price-point needs to be well structured to attract suitors. But if you work the angles right, cross promotion can be a startup's best friend—adding some much-needed rocket fuel to your new baby.

The real secret of the Daily Deal sites was that 30%-50% of people never redeem their vouchers; this is how you can end up making the margins work after it's all said and done. So, keep that in mind if you can find one that's still sending out emails to perspective buyers. Oh yeah, nobody told you? None of these sites send out emails to clients anymore, so they have all pretty much turned into glorified shopping websites that are always running the massive 50-percent-off, red-tag, sale. A modality previously reserved to sad desperation attempts such as clearance sales, outlet malls, or other fire-sale type offerings. It's like the storefront that always has the going-out-of-business sign out front, but they never go out of business. Ask me why they have done this and I would not have a good answer for you. And if you can't say something nice, it's best not to say anything at all!

Many businesses found out that hard way that most Daily Deals customers are usually one-night-stand affairs, so you shouldn't expect any of them to stick around and cook you breakfast the next day. They got what they wanted and have moved on. They are like the Vikings of the consumer world...consume, destroy, and repeat. People have also accused Groupon of putting people out of business by flooding them with uncanny amounts of traffic, effectively overloading the startups that are just trying to break even. Even though their program amounts to little more than glorified ad-budget loan-sharking, it has still given many businesses a shot at the big time. Business deals will always come with their fair share of risk and Groupon isn't putting a gun to anyone's head—so I say for a small startup it can sometimes represent a gamble that worth the risk.

Being someone who has dealt with the majority of these Daily Deals companies personally, there seems to be a tendency for business owners to get steamrolled from the Daily Deal sales people. People get a little too excited and start acting like new-car buyers, failing to do their due diligence. Always keep in mind that they need you as much as you need them; you should never let them steamroll you into accepting terms that you're not comfortable with. It's up to you as the business owner to treat the Daily Deal contract negotiations like any other form of sales deal. If they hand you some terms you think will endanger your long-term stability, you shouldn't do it.

All drawbacks aside, being able to generate hype for your startup with no upfront costs was an amazing thing—and something that many people have underestimated. You have to give credit where credit is due; had Groupon not come into existence, many startups would have never had a chance to succeed. Without Groupon, they would not have been able to effectively raise the advertising budget to reach that many potential customers at one time. Granted, to be eligible for said services, your business has to be somewhat established; but, really, it doesn't take that long to meet their consideration requirements.

Groupon effectively turned mass discounting into something trendy. These mass group purchases opened the door for every area of business to be able to shift into using the economy of scale to turn a profit. Granted, it's a challenging scenario in many ways; fulfilling thousands upon thousands of orders in a 60- to 180-day window is no easy task. I personally can't wait until this model spreads into other areas of business, such as DVD sales, book sales, art sales, and the like. Flooding the market with your fresh product can be a good turn-and-burn scenario to make some quick volume revenue.

Although the thrifty shoppers out there might still be singing the praises of such long-term trends, as a business owner it makes it much more difficult to focus on quality control. Quality of products, services, and customer service can all suffer when you're operating at capacity and serving customers below cost. Conversely, there's always a chance for the upsell, however remote it may be.

In times past it might have taken 6 months to 2 years to generate that amount of foot traffic into a fledgling enterprise. So, if you have a really fresh viral concept, you stand to do well despite any short-term setbacks. Obviously, from a pricing standpoint you may only break even for the first few months, or perhaps even lose a few bucks, but after that it should be downhill. Sadly, many businesses developed a cross promotional addiction, relying on that revenue for a primary source of income. I would be careful with this model personally, as I don't see it as a sustainable model unless you have a highly unconventional business model.

Remember: the main purpose of cross promotion is to use another business' advertising budget to create some cheap publicity for your business, effectively growing your reach and your media following. You should always encourage your customers to spread the love by checking in on foursquare, snapping shots with Instagram, tweeting about their trip, etc. Next thing you know, you will have yourself a *bonafide* viral marketing campaign, all for a fraction of the normal price some fancy PR firm would charge. Utilizing a little bit of DIY, and perhaps coaxing yourself a local intern, you should be good to go.

Now, if you're looking for high-end clientele, cross promotion might not be the ticket; but, if you are looking to find cheap exposure at another business' expense, it can be a powerful win-win. These cross promotions can garner you some yelp reviews and some good old-fashioned word-of-mouth advertising, all of which are worth their weight in gold. When you have a competitive platform to boost your online reviews, you can then use that as a bargaining chip in other areas as well. This, in turn, will help your overall webpage rankings by boosting your traffic stats and your auxiliary search relevancy. Combine that with a killer SEO guy and you have a recipe for success. When it comes to branding, the more publicity you can garner the better; publicity becomes your leverage for generating even larger cross-promotional opportunities and turning other companies' marketing dollars into your own. These are all major keys to get your phones ringing and to starting to build a more lucrative, and more permanent, clientele.

Morphing the Daily Deals model

As platforms such as Groupon, IndieGogo, Kickstarter, and Living Social become more desperate to differentiate——and turn a profit—they will be forced to incorporate a wide range of yet-unavailable product offerings. A process that is well underway, considering the current array of charitable offerings and other unique "crowd" services popping up daily. I predict that as time goes on, and as the economy tightens up for the next few years, we will see this model creep into many other area of business. This will happen as the larger corporations struggle to stay afloat due to higher taxes and lower revenues in certain areas. Just as www.opentable.com allows you to book a restaurant table at any place in town that has an open seat, soon you will be able to get open seats on a plane, same day, for a fraction of the price. Perhaps coffee shops will start renting out workstations. IPhone apps will be sold in a Groupon-type fashion for a fraction of the normal price. I'm sure that major universities, or at least online universities, will consider this as well.

No one wants to admit it, but as things tighten up, so too shall bigger businesses need to squeeze dimes out of nickels to stay afloat. Think about this: take a company like Wal-Mart, which operates on a 5% margin; thereby, relying on mass volume to make their money. This means that if Walmart loses 5% of their clientele for their big box stores, they would quickly be in the red; hence, it doesn't take many people to make a big change in the economic landscape of this country. We as enlightened human beings are supremely capable of creating any economic system that we want. This means acting like adults and taking responsibility for all of our economic decisions and supporting the types of businesses that you would like to see flourish—and boycotting those you want to go away. As is the case with Walmart and other similar chains, sometimes the lowest costs can have the highest vocational price. Again, no one has a gun to these people's head, but it's still worth noting we should always economically support those with an ethical business model when at all possible.

Benefits of crowdfunding for startups of the future

What does that mean for the current small business? Well, say you are aiming to produce low-cost computer chairs that have some sort of new and novel function. Perhaps these computer chairs are able to block out EMFs, as well as sync up to your computer via Bluetooth speakers in the headrests. Whatever your product may be, through these new startup mechanisms you will be able to obtain enough upfront sales to effectively self-fund, or "bootstrap" (to finance yourself using only your own capital), your operation. Being able to produce things at an economy of scale that makes it feasible for you to operate without taking any heavy upfront risks has already started to redefine the startup model. With businesses requiring less and less risk on the part of the entrepreneur, we will begin to see a massive resurgence in the entrepreneurial field within the coming years. Not having to run at a financial loss for years at the outset is a huge change for the business world. We have yet to see its full effects in action due to increased taxation and other negative economic factors. In essence, crowdfunding will reduce the fear factor surrounding starting your own business.

I predict that in the future startups will be able to get off the ground in weeks instead of months; and become profitable in months instead of years. Not to say that time and effort should not go into preparation. But all of the time that used to be spent begging for money and trying to convince dozens of angel investors and equity groups about your novel ideas can be repurposed to your benefit––effectively giving you less hassle and more energy, which will get you off the ground sooner. On a grassroots level, all you will really have to do is:

- ✓ Produce some quality marketing materials.
- ✓ Get the word out to the right startup market!
- ✓ Develop a solid brand growth strategy.
- ✓ Offer enough evidence to a crowdfunding site to prove that you could actually manufacture said products or services.

If you can do these three things, you will be off and running. With less moaning and more doing, kids could quickly get off the ground with innovative art, music, or public works via talents. Parents could raise money for their kid's college based on pledging meritorious deeds for the community. We could be hiring out teams of youth to clean up graffiti and plant trees in under-forested areas. It may even make sense for Gen-Y entrepreneurs to support other Gen-Y businesses. It's hard to say how many applications this new wave of businesses might have.

START-UP FEVER

Perhaps we could have an Angel List-type system for retired people who would like to pick up odds-and-ends work. Screw going to India, why not hire Pa-Pa and Gramma. Many of our seniors are struggling to eke out a living on social security and would sorely appreciate some side work that can be done remotely—or through some form of traditional written correspondence.

As a brief aside, did you know that seniors are not allowed to make more than two thousand a month or they will not qualify for their social security checks in many cases? This is just one more way the government encourages people to be less than productive. How ludicrous is this? Obviously, our entire governmental structure would probably be running much more efficiently if we were able to enlist the help of these veterans of life. Again, if you want to discard decades of pragmatic world experience and wisdom, then go ahead—but I know that there are very capable, brilliant, seniors who are being over looked due to ageism. Everyone has to hustle and you don't know what cards someone has been dealt in his or her life. Perhaps they have had a very difficult financial run-in with medical problems or a divorce settlement gone wrong. Who are we to judge older people and automatically assume that they cannot manage money and are therefore undeserving of employment and our respect?

The more that we can diversify the labor pool, the better off we will be. Many older Americans may seem set in their ways, but perhaps this is due to the fact that they have lived long enough to discover a way of life that is useful to them; therefore, they've adopted a "if it isn't broke, don't fix it" kind of attitude. Obviously, they are not necessarily a "tech sector" asset, but who cares.

America still needs many other tasks done and perhaps there is some creative mojo left in that population segment. I'm sure they have seen enough nonsensical governmental bumbling to adequately prescribe fixes to some of our big government woes. I would imagine that perhaps seniors are frowned upon because the corporate world does not view them as "easily programmable" little drones, which is sad. Perhaps they will change their mind when a few seniors start to enact programs like these themselves in a few years, when the internet-active group of older folks hit the scene. Utilizing new crowdfunding models, no individual should be considered obsolete, as the individuals in society are able to readily define their own preferred work based on their own intrinsic knowledge of themselves—and their abilities.

Startup School

Businesses of the future will no longer need to rely on the slow-to-react methodologies of the past, as they will be forced by their client base to explore new avenues of approach much more frequently. Establishing small business network partnerships with smaller suppliers around the country, changes will happen much faster than they did a decade ago. This also forces traditionally stable markets into uncertain territory. The way I see it, the business cycle will start to run hot to cold much faster in the future. As the dinosaurs start to adapt or die off, the rules will change. Companies will have to constantly be on guard for smaller fish cutting into their market share. Hopefully, America will become less dependent on attorneys and more driven by a healthy sense of entrepreneurial competition! Again, we can't expect all of this to change overnight, but the post-digital world will have its upsides.

Trade schools might be able to replace some of the useless AA and business bachelor programs of Middle America. Perhaps we will develop some form of universities on YouTube: compiling the millions of hours of DIY projects available and somehow creating valid skill sets for the future. Kids could teach other kids online without time gaps in useable practices. Obviously, one of the main problems of the collegiate educational system remains in its time relevance. In a world where business practices change drastically every five years, college-level information becomes irrelevant quickly. Of course, corporate America loves them some college grads, as they have already proven themselves malleable to formulaic regimentation. Once they have been taught how to learn in the linear, hyper-focused, college approach, corporate training is easier than with the undisciplined, rebellious, high school graduate crowd. Despite being somewhat creatively shutdown at the behest of the public school system, many of the younger generations are just too bored with corporate jobs to make good employees. Most of the modern youth is grossly overstimulated and has spent very little time in nature, in which they could process the insanity of growing up as a human being. Being unable to cope with the vast amounts of seemingly nonsensical phenomenon happening in the outside world, the mind starts to suffer from conditions such as ADD and the like. You can easily equate this to a car engine that has been left on too long. If you run a car for four days straight without sufficient fuel or rest, it would easily start to overheat or malfunction in some other way.

If America is serious about restarting the economy, they will get even more serious about teaching kids functional skill sets that they can go out and use right out of high school; skill sets that encourage a problem-solving, entrepreneurially adaptable, mindset. Theoretically, we could place kids in different kinds of trade schools, or other small business classes, that could kick-start their entrepreneurial careers right out of high school. Common sense would say that we should demystify the average life a drug dealer (and other criminal trades as well) so people can see the truly demonic impact of these nefarious lifestyles in society. I love the one Ted Talk that broke down the statistics around being a crack dealer and how the average street dealer makes 3-4 dollars an hour, while the local drug lord makes 100k or above. Not only do you make terrible money dealing crack on a low level, the mortality rates are off the chart.

I feel like the whole country needs to see videos like these that describe how utterly destructive drug dealing is to the fabric of society. Even as an end user, drug addicts end up supporting an industry with absolutely zero value creation. Drugs are sadly one of the main pillars upon which America has been built; and if we are not careful, they will destroy us from the inside out like a virus. If someone would have shown that Ted Talk to the two-bit drug dealers in my high school, they may have started prepping a resume for their local fast food joint.

Instead of being real with kids, we try to scare kids by bringing cops into schools and having them detail all of the mind-altering effects that these drugs might have; a very odd approach if I do say so myself. Kids are smart and many of them are also smartasses. I have found it best to just get to the point and tell them like it is; otherwise, we are just sheltering them in unhealthy ways. Every child is different. But emotionally fragile as they are, if they don't understand the real perils of the world, we will end up with another crop of emotionally uninvolved perpetual high-schoolers that we are stuck with today!

Kids need to be made aware of how pointless and demonstrable the life of a two-bit drug dealer is. They should also be made aware how horrifying it is to know that you have destroyed all of your "customer's" lives in the process. Risking your entire livelihood while condemning people to perpetual escapism through living in alternate realities never seemed like a good career option to me. Obviously, movies do a good job of glorifying this lifestyle. And drugs sell themselves as they say; so wherever an escapist person exists, drugs won't be far behind.

We must take things back to their source; America was founded with many people having no education at all. Strangely, this street smart brand of Americana bred a much more successful economy than the apathetic yuppies could do in 100 years. This is a time when Americans successfully enjoyed a thriving hemp trade and personal tobacco cultivation. The crafting of fine goods was commonplace, as well as other industrial trades. As an aside, tobacco in its pure form does have some spiritual characteristics and might represent a useful tool for communicating with your higher self in a ritualistic way. This is if you can get any of the pure tobacco that has been all but outlawed here in the states. There are also many other forms of natural drug detoxes, such as Abogaine and others, which have been lobbied out of legality as well.

126

"The school system remained largely private and unorganized until the 1840s. Public schools were always under local control, with no federal role, and little state role. The 1840 census indicated that of the 3.68 million children between the ages of five and fifteen, about 55% attended primary schools and academies. Beginning in the late 1830s, more private academies were established for girls for education past primary school, especially in northern states. Some offered classical education similar to that offered to boys." http://en.wikipedia.org/wiki/History_of_educatio n_in_the_United_States

Yeah, you heard that right. Only 55% of kids even went to school and somehow the economy was much better during that time. Why is this you might ask? Well, perhaps it's the fact that people were too busy working and developing practical skill sets to have a formal education. Or perhaps it's fact that that pragmatic governmental officials of the time realized that it's not fiscally sound to pay for every single child to go to school. Whatever the case, having a school system that was highly decentralized meant that teachers could teach things as fast as the kids could learn them. Obviously, Abraham Lincoln comes to mind as one of the best examples of a self-starter type of child. This type of system also resulted in children being taught things that were indigenous to their particular region—and perhaps even unique to their own particular aptitudes. Teachers were also able to teach kids things that were relevant to their local customs and cultures, as well as things about the heritage of the community. If you really want to get into the nitty-gritty on how our public education system was subverted at the highest level, check out Charlotte Iserbyt's *The Deliberate Dumbing Down of America*—a phenomenal work on the subject of education.

We need to start questioning our preconceived notions that public school is some form of benevolent cure-all for society. If anything, they are teaching kids how to be codependent on a corporate system that does not have their best interests at heart. There are still good teachers out there, but the curriculum in many areas has become a far cry from balanced education—let alone dispersing any common sense or morality to the youth. This "education utopia" might have been the case 50-150 years ago, but this is far from the case today. Today's public schools are great for teaching kids how to party hard, look cool, have sex, and parrot ugly, debased, cultural rhetoric. Everyone is expected to go to college, while the colleges hoard the money and don't even spend it on the kids. How is this system supposed to fix our economy again? I'm drawing a blank.

The system is rigged to create helpless consumers and suck all the common sense and morality out of our kids by the time they hit college. Again, why do I know this? Well, I know this because I have met a good subsection of the populous that went through just such a mechanism. Unless you're shelling out $15,000 to $30,000 a year for your kid to go to high-end leaning-centric private school, your children are going to come out unprepared at best—and hating life at worst. In my estimation, nothing about public schools today necessarily helps children to find their true purpose in the world—or even lets you know that you have a purpose for that matter. You are the best student if you can memorize factual data and mind your manners and keep quiet. There are a few promising charter schools here and there, but it's not enough to stop the bleeding. We need a comprehensive, locally based, education reform movement. I'm not sure if that means homeschools, charter schools, or some mix of everything, but our kids are getting too much garbage from the media to make good decisions without a solid foundation based on reality.

It's no wonder kids are having a hard time figuring out what they want to do with their lives; they become legal adults without learning anything about the brilliant mystery of life that is all around them. Instead, we find our youth largely adrift, looking for joy in all of the escapist pursuits of the world. This does not create a culture of determined, fulfilled, working adults.

At the end of the day, it comes back to balance. Instead of having the males in our society become one-dimensional drones, or sports nuts, we need to cultivate a society that encourages people to be well rounded. The women aren't faring much better, even with higher educational status; that hasn't done much for the vicious social convention plaguing womankind. We are training girls to base their entire self-worth upon their image and their relationships. Don't worry: materialism is alive and well in the status-obsessed female culture.

During the renaissance, people were expected to be able to write literature, play music, and create art. Now, you are lucky if you drag Middle Americans out of the living room long enough to zap-fry a pop tart. Multi-skilled acculturated citizens would probably account for less than 10% of the US population in my estimation. The self-sufficient pioneering American represents a phenomenon that has not been in existence for at least 50 years. Some of the old-timers had 5-10 different valuable skill sets. Now, many city folks can barely cook a meal for themselves; instead, they call mommy and daddy when their iPhone has crashed.

This isn't about teaching everyone to live off that land, but it is about teaching people things that happen outside of a computer screen or a video game console. I would assume this is why the female culture is outpacing the males in education. They are able to differentiate themselves through their intellectual abilities, where with the males it's all about external achievement. Internal achievement is virtually nonexistent. You would have thought that humanity would have progressed to the point of using the vastly untapped resources of our psychic and metaphysical skill sets that have been seen within the leading edges of our populace (Nikola Tesla, William Blake, Edgar Cayce, etc.); but, no, we're still in the Stone Ages psychologically speaking. We are still working toward garnering some psychic sovereignty from our families, but have barely begun analyzing the mass psychosis of the tyrannical authoritarian systems worldwide.

Again, I love ogling nice cars and playing recreational sports as much as the next guy, but they don't consume my life. If I spent my entire life in front of the slave box, I doubt many people would find me interesting or engaging; yet, this is what most people aspire to do. The modern citizen is busy chasing a lifetime of perpetual relaxation. It's like the scene in "Office Space" where Peter's neighbor asks what he, Peter, would do if he had a million dollars. Peter's reply is: "I would do nothing; I would relax; I would sit on my ass all day; I would do nothing." Later in the movie Peter finds a bit more purpose, but it does go to prove an apt point about the current office culture. Couple this with the fact that I doubt our species was conceived to sit around waiting to die. Whatever happened to the element of adventure in life? When did Americans trade in the dream of an expansive and creative life for a 72" plasma screen and a couch? It's like manifest destiny happened and then everyone just wanted to quit. The lazy boy has become a lazy man.

For the detective caste amongst us, there has never been a better time to be alive; we are forced to analyze a world that has been set up to trap us. A world designed to keep us insecure and locked in our own confusion. Every day we awaken and we should realize that we are living in one of the greatest puzzles the universe has ever constructed. The closer we can become to non-tyrannical economic self-sufficiency, the faster we can pursue other areas of human development—leaving the psychological conformity and barbarism to the generations of past. As they say, knowing the problem is half the battle. My hope is that these economic ideas and tools will also present part of the solution. As was stated in the introduction, we contain the solutions to all of our own problems within ourselves. To live in perpetual fear of yourself is to condemn your own internal solution-generation mechanism and to do a disservice to your own higher spiritual self.

Ch. 7
Starting from Scratch…

The truth is, many people reading this book will have to claw their way up from the gutter, working crappy retail jobs like I did. Others will be starving themselves while going through college. Still, others will be bred into entrepreneurial success from birth by a dynamic family unit. However you get there, the suffering of the self-made entrepreneur is a form of personal penance. All of this harangue will be taken on voluntarily in hopes of realizing a personal dream out in the wide world. People think NFL players are tough. Well, you haven't seen tough until you have seen a real entrepreneur in action. Dealing with real-world crisis situations, which involve hundreds of people, is no picnic—nor is saving a company from some wolf in a suit across town who wants to rob you blind with a frivolous lawsuit. It happens all the time; and unless you're prepared for changes—good, bad, and indifferent—you will have a hard time hacking it out there. Anyone who has run his or her own shop for an extended period of time knows that Murphy's Law always applies.

The more money you have, the bigger target you become. That's just the brass tacks; and this why the spiritually superior man strives to have just enough. Not as many people are willing to steal from the man who has just enough—nor steal from a man who is naturally generous with others. Even though amassing a fortune for yourself makes you a bit of a target, that doesn't mean we should have to withdraw from the business world entirely. Instead, perhaps we should learn to temper our conduct. If we can do that, we can lessen the motives other people may have to attack us.

But before we go into the far reaches of economic futurism, I feel it necessary to preface my unique viewpoint by shedding some light on the roots of my personal journey; a journey that took me from the depths of utter egotistical delusion to a course of steady personal progress. I'm sure that at the beginning, I was hoping to find enough cash to find a beautiful wife and settle down by the beach with a nice little family on the water. Not working but one or two days a week and having the rest of my time to be able to party it up and enjoy the best tunes, food, and cars that money could buy. I didn't really know why I wanted to have all this stuff, but to my young mind it just seemed like the thing to do because everybody wants this kind of stuff, right? Wrong, I was totally wrong; and I had no idea what would make me happy and as a result I spent years of my life chasing after other people's dreams in vain, never believing in my own dreams or strategies enough to implement them within my life. Utterly depressed, I had no idea how to find my own purpose or something worth fighting for in my life. Instead, I had given up by default, living the life of the common trite, insecure, and social climber–inherently looking to others to define my self-worth.

I was trying to control my life the conventional way, assuming that if I went out there and put on a smile, went to the right parties, and schmoozed with the right people that I would be able to easily achieve my dreams. I was a likeable guy and who wouldn't want to share their cash and prosperity with a fun party guy? Apparently, as it turns out, many people in life never really learn how to share. That simple lesson that many kids are supposed to learn in kindergarten never really seeps in; instead, people in the world operate on a mentality of economic scarcity. Feeling that if they hoard all of their money, they will find security; and if they keep tight reigns on who they let succeed around them, then they can maintain control in their lives—recreating the dictatorial behavior of the parents or bosses who had lorded over them in times past. These are things I had no clue about and, ultimately, caused my naïve level of optimism to wane later in my entrepreneurial career. But let's start at the beginning....

My quest into business began at the ripe age of seventeen. As trite as this may seem, it began when I skipped high school one day to read the book *Rich Dad Poor Dad*. This may seem like a strange contradiction of sorts, as who skips school to read a book? I wasn't exactly the most studious fellow in those days. Well for the record, I did skip school to read a book. And for me, that day was one of the most inspiring days of my young life. I realized, for the first time, that there was another way to go about defining "work." I found a way out of the rat race, where taking hell from some boss wasn't part of the long-term agenda.

One of the biggest lessons I learned from *Rich Dad Poor Dad* was the importance of running an upstanding and ethical business with good principles behind it. Looking back, even though *Rich Dad Poor Dad* had lit a fire under my backside to go out and change my life, I felt something was missing from the message. In my view, the book failed to explain how important it is that you start a business for the right reasons. Although the book was incredibly effective for gathering motivation, it also seemed like the book was merely pandering to the American "early retirement dream" or as I like to call it: the existential abyss. Whatever name you choose, I feel that Americans newfound obsession with a cushy early-retirement-type existence is a dangerous mentality that has landed us in the economic hot water that we are in. This mentality has created a business culture in which everyone mails it in at the end of his or her career in order to retire early. Many times this involves hanging co-workers, employees, and the American public out to dry in the process.

To its credit, *Rich Dad Poor Dad* did speak out against the practice of overleveraging your resources in order to start a business that you really cannot afford. I have been in the business world long enough to know that many business owners constantly operate at a deficit; when they go bust, the employees get left holding the bag. In fact, many of the worst ideologically toxic corporations are actually cash poor and way overleveraged on their assets. If you can't honestly afford your employees—and are supporting your business paycheck to paycheck—you really shouldn't be in business. You should stop and really re-think your business model before you start destroying other people's lives. You have every right to destroy your own life, but not that of anyone else. These non-cash-generating-finance-only businesses represent a large portion of the derivatives bubble as well.

Just for an example, Clear Channel Inc. is a corporation that has taken over seventy percent of the radio stations in the US; and is 22 billion dollars in debt. Yet, we still get atrociously trite and uninspired musical artists. How is this possible? Again we come back to the theory of when things are artificially propped up instead of being allowed to die gracefully, they breed stagnation. Crowdfunding will help to get away from this financing-everything model. It will help to create some quantifiable liquidity, as well as economic accountability, within new small businesses. Speaking of the devil, someone should crowd-fund a radio station! How cool would that be?

Wheel of fortune

The way I look at reincarnation is a constant recreation of different parts of the human soul. We will choose to manifest in this way or that way depending on what we want to achieve and how far we are willing to go to make changes to our soul. Businesses are no different; they are concepts that have always existed in our subconscious, but need to be brought to light by our ego-selves in order to be fully understood within the context of our current incarnation. Obviously, this whole soul-manifestation concept is one of the most complex spiritual topics ever to be pondered, but I do believe we need to drudge up some deep knowledge to solve some of these complex external problems.

During my teens, I was more focused on making a few bucks to get out of my parents' house than on building some economic empire. After working more subpar retail jobs than I can count, my prime directive was set on finding a more meaningful enterprise. I needed something that I could hang my hat on—something that could define my life. What do they call that again? Oh yeah, a vocation. Although most of my dispensable income was still devoted to partying on the weekends, I began to realize that this cycle of repetitive low-paying gigs couldn't go on forever. It was time to take matters into my own hands and try my hand at starting a business.

At the time, my mother had likewise jumped on the entrepreneurship bandwagon. After having had her fair share of strife within corporate America, she took it upon herself to develop a concierge service startup. Her newfound dream was called The Concierge Crew. The idea was to have a mobile crew to run errands for people in hotels: dog walking, dry cleaning, etc. She ended up pitching her new service to garner a contract at a major hotel in downtown Fort Worth, Texas. Even though it was ultimately unsuccessful, her plight was inspiring to me. She had enlisted help from the local Small Business Association, who helped her to put together a respectable business plan. As she had not majored in business, or had much experience in the startup world, I thought her efforts were very admirable.

Years later, when I started Digital Ascent Marketing, I would learn for myself just how difficult it is to pitch new concepts to hotels; and the amount of red tape she faced made her business a tricky one to launch. I had a hell of a time trying to pitch hotels my new concept. Even with a proven web-commercial model, which had created massive revenue increases in my test markets, the hotels' infinite bureaucracy continually stonewalled me. I would have had a better shot selling Post-It notes to the White House. Even though I produced a few good-sized deals, eventually I got tired of making cold calls and pulling teeth for chicken feed. So, I shut it down. Retrospectively, I have much sympathy for good ideas falling upon the ears of deaf bureaucracies, like what happened with my mom's venture. Luckily, her attempt did lead me to start brewing startup ideas in my own little noodle.

Soon after her foray into The Concierge Crew, my mom had also begun working on investing in off-shore real estate, which included educating herself on international tax law. Both were topics that were fascinating to me at the time. After doing a little research, my mother and I began to realize that at the highest levels, the economic system was rigged. Corporations with the mega-millions were paying no taxes; thereby, leaving the middle-class shmucks to pick up the tab. This whole process is reasonably well known in 2014; but in 2004, it was virtually unknown to the common citizen.

Obviously, I don't think that these tax policies are fair by any means, but tax-avoidance schemes are nothing new. Hell, America was founded on tax evasion and with good reason might I add! Through this investor network, we had discovered how these mega-investors were funneling money through three to four countries and paying effectively no taxes as a result. But even if you wanted to pull off that type of tax scheme for yourself, you will probably never have enough cash to actually do it. Things like that take a small army of accountants, as well as bankers in other countries, and lots of legwork. Really, it has just made me realize that the money game changes the further you get up the ladder.

I will be leaving the balance of that subject for your own research, but just realize that tax rackets like this do exist; Apple Inc. is living proof. Although they are by no means the worst of the mega-corporations, the US and EU both charged them with paying effectively no international corporate taxes. Honestly, there was nothing illegal about what they did, as this is par for the course in corporate America—especially when you are making that kind of money. We all should know by now that life isn't fair, but that doesn't mean you shouldn't get out there and throw your hat into the ring. Many big things grow from humble beginnings.

The purpose of this book is not to provide a rose-colored dissertation on how easy entrepreneurial life is, as that would be a fallacy. In my estimation, entrepreneurial life should only be pursued by those who want to truly challenge themselves on all levels. The world needs more people who are passionately dedicated to being a positive agent for human development in the business world. When you start your own operation in the external world, you also simultaneously awaken the shadow self's countermeasures as well. It's like the universe knows you're about to do something great, so it feels the need to put you through your paces.

Wax on-Wax off

My aim from seventeen-years-old onward was to become entirely "boss free" in my work life; that didn't really pan out within my ideal timeline. Eight years and five businesses later, I had finally reached my goal. Luckily, by the time I was twenty I was working as a freelancer, so I wasn't totally a slave to the man. I really enjoyed that time, as it taught me a strong work ethic and showed me how I could one day gain control over my vocational existence. I also know that crowdfunding naturally breeds more freelance-type environments that will also help to change the vocational landscape long term—encouraging more independence and smaller working groups in many cases.

Psychologically speaking, freelancing is much healthier in my estimation, as it teaches you self-control and self-discipline—both of which can be avoided within many traditional "jobs." In a traditional "job," you force a boss to take on this parental role; thereby, further instilling the perpetual codependency imbued within our societal structure. Even though learning to get up at a reasonable hour and knock out a long to-do list can be a daunting task, flying solo is still a great feeling. At the beginning, cultivating a high level of self-discipline is no picnic. But, eventually, it will help you develop a healthy sense of pride by knowing that you are able to accomplish so many things on your own. All stress aside, freelancing also helps the economy to naturally breed better working conditions. When you are freelancing, you are able to choose when and where you work. So, if you're unhappy about your working conditions, you only have yourself to blame.

Many of these new startups can be handled on a project-by-project basis, where employees freely move from one company to the next to meet the demands of the current project. This is also one of the beautiful things about working in Los Angeles. Most of the entertainment industry works on a freelance basis. As the saying goes in Hollywood, "You truly are only as good as your last gig." If you treat people like hell or cop a *prima donna* attitude, there are usually repercussions for that nonsense—which is why it's possible to get permanently black-balled in this city. Freelancing helps to ensure this happens, since it places more emphasis on professional reputations!

Freelancing also dispenses with a good amount of un-needed bureaucracy. Sadly, self-governance is not something everyone is capable of, so it will never be for everyone; but something is better than nothing. Self-motivation is something that is relatively uncommon in a culture stricken with the "early retirement mentality" and narcissistic self-indulgence. Self-discipline can be a chore to cultivate when you don't have a structured framework as a kid, but I can assure you it's possible. I am living proof that it can be done.

During my younger jack-of-all-trades phase, I worked somewhere in the neighborhood of thirty jobs—a figure I think might have set a record. I have done everything from sales to construction to fast food to lighting to producing commercials. As you have might have guessed: due to the high number of jobs, I was a sterling employee—at least until I got bored. If there is one thing that *Rich Dad Poor Dad* had taught me, it was that you should work to learn not to just earn a paycheck. So, I did just that. I went out and worked every odd job that I could find. Little did I realize that I was actually building an invaluably eclectic skill set at the same time. This phase lasted from the ages of fourteen to twenty-six, when I finally transitioned into full-time self-employment. Granted, not many people can become full-time entrepreneurs at sixteen. I was still mad at myself for having taken so long. This is something I eventually learned to let go of, as everything happens in due time. By working in all manner of different occupations, I learned the good, the bad, and the ugly of corporate America in an up-close-and-personal manner. Without my vocational obstacles, perhaps I would not have been able to create such innovative solutions to my problems later on.

Even though it took me eight years of fiscal/spiritual/emotional struggle, looking back I would not want it any other way. The mistakes of my past can be written off as a healthy process of deconstruction within my own life; a process that led me to build the spiritual fortitude I would need later in life. Those who know more must do more; and failure teaches you a hell of a lot more than success. Now, in my defense, I would say that in regards to financial luck and education, I had to start at the rock bottom. Neither of my parents was any good at saving money; that's why they had me to spend it all for them, right? I was actually much worse than either of them at saving money. If it didn't have to do with blowing cash in some sort of weekend free-for-all, I wasn't interested.

Along with my poor money management skills, I was also commitment-phobic of the business world. I would dabble in this and dabble in that, until I lost interest—at which point I would move on. My roving eye would generally kick in around the six-month marker and I would start looking for some other hill to climb or a new ditch to dig. Some are born with silver spoons in hand; but me, I was born with a shovel at the bottom of a ditch. All joking aside, I really do believe that most other peoples' karma will make it much easier for them to start a business than it was for me; apparently, I like learning things the hard way. I am also sure that there will also be many people out there will have a more difficult path than me as well and my heart goes out to them. Life is never predictable, as every individual's journey is as unique as every star in the sky.

Having made every mistake under the sun, I eventually developed a sure footing with which to commence my vocational life. Being unhindered by many of the greenhorn problems, I can now look back and laugh at my personal pain and poverty, as the joke really was on me. Alien robot zombies attacking, you say? No problem. Black plague resurgence? (*Yawn*) Indefinite worldwide electronics blackout? Don't make me laugh. After what I went through, no matter what the universe is cooking up for planet Earth, I will be ready for anything.

START-UP FEVER

Redefining Success

No matter what your starting point may be, vocational success is still possible. Success is nebulous term, as it means different things to different people. For me, success was not and will never be a monetary thing. I may end up with millions of dollars at some point, but in the words of the rapper Biggie Smalls, "Mo Money, Mo Problems." Anyone wanting to rule the world must realize that it's a 24/7 job to run an empire. Remember when ships get old: they all start to spring leaks. I personally enjoy having the time in my day to help others and contemplate the deeper issues of life. Upper management is a taxing place to be in many ways, since you can spend your whole life solving other people's problems. During all the hustle and bustle of solving everybody else's problems, you can forget to learn about yourself, which is the most important task of all.

Is this to say that I don't enjoy working on large projects? No, I just don't have a need to maintain a public façade of decadence, as there are many people out there who are concentrating on that aspect of human life. I say good luck to them on their quest. But if I wanted to make a rap video out of my life, I would make one. For me, as long as I eat well, have my good health, and projects I'm passionate about, then I'm as happy as a clam. Over the course of my evolving career, I have seen many clients and friends alike get in touch with their own internal muse, their true self, their prime directive so to speak: a process that helped them all to generate massive success. For those willing to dig deep and make big internal changes, the rewards are priceless. So, if at first you don't understand yourself, try, try, again!

It always serves to remember the fact that you may lose interest in projects along the way—not to mention relationships. Many times, just as my businesses would start to become profitable, I would turn tail and run headlong into something else that seemed a bit more challenging. For me, startup life wasn't about the money as much as the thrill of the hunt. Often, I was stricken with business partners or colleagues who were unwilling to make personal changes, which halted the growth of the business. This is always a tough scenario. Obviously, forcing people to change is impossible, but shutting down a business is also rough.

In retrospect, even though I had an unconventional approach, this wasn't a bad thing. I was subconsciously forcing myself to expand my skill set since I would not allow intellectual stagnation in my work. Even though these processes were painful and involved a good amount of self-sabotage, at the end of the day, they were a productive phase of my journey. Sometimes, life requires you to bleed for your progress; and sometimes, it just bleeds your wallet. Despite some pre-mature balding and a chain-smoking habit I had to kick, I feel like I got away pretty much unscathed from my time in start-up hell.

Hidden Hiccups

Surprisingly, my entrepreneurial quest ended up stretching into every area of my life. Most notably, I was forced to dig into the areas of psychological and spiritual development. These were two areas that I never would have considered exploring in the early stages of my life. Although I felt that I was a spiritual person in some capacity, I really didn't know much about it. I just felt sorry for myself and figured the world owed me a paycheck for having to go through all the drama of my childhood. Again, I was busy partying morning 'til night; what use would I have for spiritual development? Let alone figuring out that I would need to clean up my karmic patterns before I could start to have success in my ventures; being blind to the source of my repeated self-sabotage attempts eventually led to the realization that I was handicapped from the outset.

As it turned out, my subconscious mind was trying to undo every good thing that I did for myself and force me back into the same old lifestyle I had always known. Most people are addicted to their own breed of insanity, and I was no different. Luckily, I had the balls to man up and face the fact that I had to change some things if I was ever going to blaze a different trail than those around me. Of course, this really all started to turn around until after the death of my father. Something sketchy happens when you lose a loved one that instills a deep sense of hope, along with a healthy sense of existential paranoia. However disturbing and tragic it was, at least I had the common sense to use the tragedy as inspiration to start getting my life in order.

It seemed that this jump-switch started with quitting cigarettes, the definitive exercise in self-discipline and self-control. After that, it was smoking weed and, finally, alcohol. Oh yes, I was a pothead alright and unashamed about it. I really thought there was a light at the end of that tunnel, but it turned out that was just a train headed to run me over. A train that was running on one bong load's worth of fuel at a time. I'm sure that many entrepreneurs out there probably maintain some of these addictions to cope with the stressors of work life; and I can't say that I blame them. It's the old work-hard-play-hard mantra. But for me, this strategy was just inefficient and psychologically distressing. Seeking balance from external sources will always be an unsustainable model in my book; but again, to each their own.

I recently watched a documentary about a Buddhist teacher who tricked a bunch of hippies into bringing in their drugs to the spiritual class he was teaching, only to burn all the drugs in front of them while chanting: "we are burning our self-deception." This struck me as a powerful phrase; it has stuck with me. Life is tough enough when you do know what's happening, let alone when you blind yourself to the truth of what you're up against. There's no need to judge a process; it's simply about finding out what works for you and running with it.

For me, all of these things only served to chain me to the unhealthy societally conformist patterns—patterns that kept me running in circles. It probably took me four to five years to get off that stuff. I honestly could not have done it without my Buddhist chanting practice. Originally, that is what helped me develop my inner spiritual fortitude, but later on I found other practices as well. Spirituality can be the most individualistic thing in the world, although mainstream religion would have you believe the exact opposite. Long story short, spirituality is a private enterprise; and however you choose to go about it is your business and no one else's. If you choose to share your spiritual insights with others, then it's on you if it's not well received. Being that politics and spirituality are some of the most divisive issues, I generally find it best to let people grapple with those topics on the micro level. Proselytizing always seemed like a lesson in futility to me. Even though my spiritual practices definitively changed my life, I know that no two people will ever have the exact same experience. For me, chanting gave me the courage and the patience to become a better person and to leave my old ways behind. It allowed me to cultivate spiritual focus and shed light upon the true causes for my mishaps. The kicker is very interesting because although it was obviously in my karma for all of these things to have a place in my life, many of these addictions and social norms were not even my own. I began to understand how I had absorbed these unhealthy traits subconsciously from others.

When we are young, our brains are totally pure and absorbing information at a million miles a minute. If your parents suffered from money problems when you were young, then there's a good chance that you will as well. Being that this erroneous poverty mentality gets lodged in our subconscious, it really becomes a bugger to get rid of. There are a few ways to tackle it, but I will leave that to more competent healers to discuss. A lot of this pre-programed failure lies within the pre-rational stages of subconscious development; hence, the logic-based adult mind has problems identifying these root issues. This is because the issues came about before any logic was in place to tell your infantile mind that you were not also suffering from economic problems. You were just a little sponge soaking up both the noble traits and the hidden problems in your family.

Imagine that most people's deepest psychological stumbling blocks actually start when they are very young. Who would have thought? Still, that just doesn't seem fair! As when you are young, the emotional developmental sectors of your psyche also lack any form of emotional shielding. These childhood problems can wreak havoc for people in adulthood, where the loop perpetuates! As much as we strive to be different than our parents, we can end up repeating their same mistakes if we don't take the time to heal the underlying issues.

Time for a Vocation

Having chased down many dead-end dreams, I began to realize that you need more than passion and a fiscal dream to be successful. Your business must include something that will intimately harness your unique skill set. It needs to incorporate something only you can bring to the table, something that no other Tom, Dick, or Harry can do. This serves multiple purposes. Not only does it keep you engaged in your career over the long haul, but it also creates internally based job security. So, hypothetically speaking, should someone come along that was aiming to take over your gig in the workplace, you would be covered. With a true vocation, you will know beyond a shadow of a doubt that no one will ever be able to perform your job the way that you can.

Will there ever be a true replacement to Steve Jobs? Howard Hughes? Michael Jackson? Elvis? I think not. No one could ever take the place of these cultural giants. This is because their vocation was an extension of their higher spiritual purpose. These types of people have truly transcended insecurity and allowed us to share in their soul's unique gifts. Obviously, it's easy to point at a celebrity and say: "If I just had some of that pizazz or if I had their brains, etc." But really, even if you are a common day laborer, if you perform your duties with your whole heart and soul, the universe will take notice and good things will ensue. The magic comes from your belief in yourself and the realization that you are serving a larger purpose in the cosmos. If you are continually cultivating your gifts, you can rest assured that you will be prepared when the time is right. No matter how bad your luck may or may not be, everyone gets at least a couple good opportunities in his or her lifetime. Small successes almost always snowball into big successes. Plus, everyone respects someone who is constantly improving himself or herself, no matter what his or her station in life. In the words of Laozi:

> "When you are content to be simply yourself and don't compare or compete, everyone will respect you." Laozi, *Tao Te Ching*

The lack of motivation within so many individuals in society will always perplex me. Perhaps it is due to the consensus trance or the media or the religions or the government—or perhaps it's just a sense of existential hopelessness. Usually you can find these purposeless, vocation-less, creatures stumbling home late at night, trying to party harder than the night before—succinctly showing the world how badass they are at running away. The prospect of change is paralyzing in the eyes of the fragile ego; hence, most people never find their vocation. Were they perpetually dedicated to figuring out *who* and *what* they really were, then, by default, their vocation would actually start to find them. Whatever the cause for this may be, it's always good to realize the unlimited inherent potential within humanity. To use an example: if we traded in every drug dealer for a rocket scientist, all of us would probably be driving anti-gravity space-cars by now.

Think about it: we are born on Earth and for the first three to four years of our lives we have almost no control over ourselves or anything within our environment. We are almost totally helpless if left to our own devices. Isn't that a perplexing phenomenon within itself? I'm not sure I want to be totally helpless and wake up in a foreign place again, so how can I avoid this? What is the purpose of that helplessness? What is the function of a child then? Who are your parents? Why did you choose them to be your parents? Or why did they choose you? Or was it all just some coincidence? What did you dream about at that age? When did you first think about a job? Perhaps these questions will give you some sort of a clue or at least provide you with a vehicle to start a meaningful internal dialogue.

I'm pretty sure no little kid grows up thinking about working as an accountant or a middle manager. Nor does any kid dream about working in a cubicle or staring at a computer screen for ten hours a day. How has most of humanity come to think these are the good jobs? Looking out into the beauty and complex interconnectedness that composes nature, one must realize that there are better ways to make a living. There must be a sustainable economic system that enables us to live a more centered existence.

Left to their own devices, I doubt that children would naturally gravitate toward television. I believe this is merely the monkey-see-monkey-do effect taking over. Since they see mommy and daddy being cool and watching the old slave box, they want to be cool, too! Again, there is nothing inherently wrong with any piece of technology, as it just represents a tool. The problem comes when we engage these tools without using proper discernment.

Television represents a process of programming with no reciprocal input. Basically, you are not allowed to talk back and tell the TV what you think. This is a problem. If you are not informed enough to understand what your subconscious is seeing when you are watching the device, and since many of the messages are downright evil, you are being programmed to be that way as well. If you could see through all of the advertising and subliminal messaging contained within, then you might start to see your television in a different light. You might see something that sparks an original idea that forces you out into the real world. But, inherently, the TV is set up to instill social convention. Vocations are totally idiosyncratic, so following the crowd will never help you find it. Collectivist activity such as this only serves to further bury our true purpose deeper within ourselves—making it harder and harder for us to find the things that will bring us true fulfillment!

Can't live with 'em, can't live without 'em

Being alone is a great thing. Don't ever let anyone tell you otherwise; because while you are alone, you have a chance to get to know your inner self. People generally are more afraid of themselves than anyone else around them. If this weren't the case, then people would have no problems mustering the courage to change their ways. Nor would they have any issue overcoming their personal insecurities. As any casual student of psychology will tell you, this is not the case. The question that we must start to address is: if you are afraid of yourself, then who is not to fear?

A quick note to all potential daters out there: having a significant other can be an expensive enterprise. It can also severely limit your time management abilities. I generally find that either totally single, or married entrepreneurs, fair best.

Starting a new venture and maintaining a new relationship can be extremely taxing in today's world. Relationships can also hamper your emotional equilibrium, which can in turn lead to impulsive or irrational business decisions. I'm not saying that relationships are not valuable. I just want people to be pragmatic about their decisions. As entrepreneurs, we must realize that there is always a tradeoff—or an opportunity cost to use the parlance of the trade. As the old cliché goes, it seems as though many of the ultra-successful corporate types can be really bad at relationships. There are many reasons for this—many of which I won't bemoan. But, ultimately, life is just a difficult balancing act. If you're trying to make hundreds of people happy at work while also trying to give undivided attention to that special someone, you might be spreading things a bit thin.

I just want to be realistic and let everyone know that the reality in life is that you can't have it all. Having the perfect fairy-tale life all the time is a delusion of the human ego. In reality, evil and destruction exists and will always represent a possible outcome, if spiritual vigilance is not maintained. Human beings are not perfect creatures, so why would our lives be perfect? Balance comes when we let go of trying to create perfection in our lives (paradoxical, I know). It just does not make much logical sense to assume in a world where we have very little control that things will magically fall into place without any hard personal development work. Earth is not supposed to be a vacation. It's a boot camp and any new-age guru who says otherwise hasn't visited the Third World lately. It's not exactly Shangri-La over there.

I feel it is a very valuable exercise for people to try and figure out if they are wired more for business or relationships and to use that self-diagnosis to try and be content with whatever momentum you already have in your life. Chasing after things is the least efficient way to reach any goal. The master strategist always lets success come to them by cultivating a sense of patience and preparing for success. This is the yin approach; something very foreign to the American hyper-extrovert-oriented mindset. With the yin approach, you put in the legwork behind the scenes and then you wait patiently. This strategy also works with relationships; if it was meant to be, it will happen. So, just let it go. This is a lot to ask for most people, as everything in society has programed us to think that we are all but useless if we are not in a relationship. No matter what you do in life, the grass will always be greener on the other side. Our job is to try and understand how to be centered during any possible scenario.

Being a little unsettled emotionally is pretty normal, so don't feel bad if you don't have everything you want— neither does most of the world! When considering relationships, we must always keep in mind that no other person in the universe can build our soul for us. Using a relationship to try to achieve personal internal development can be an uphill battle. Many times, spiritual evolution is best approached as a solo act. Most people don't trust themselves, so they are scared to be alone. They know deep down that the self-destructive urges of their shadow side could come out and haunt them at any moment. Every human being alive has the capacity for self-destruction. This is something else that I can say with great surety after working in the spiritual counseling field for some time now: people love to make things hard for themselves. Human beings are gluttons for punishment on the whole.

Ch. 8

New Crowds on the Block

Unbeknownst to many, there are other crowdfunding startups other than Kickstarter and Indiegogo that are quickly rising to prominence within the startup community. As it turns out, Los Angeles—and in particular Santa Monica (aka Silicon Beach)—is quickly becoming a *de facto* world headquarters for this unique phenomenon. The list of emerging startups in the crowdfunding sphere is quite extensive; and I am listing a few just to give you an idea of the unique angles that are currently being tested out in the marketplace. Obviously, the future will bring many variations on these business types, but I feel it's worth exploring the models already gaining traction.

First on our list is the Santa-Monica-based www.Christie Street.com; Christie Street is trying to bring a new level of sophistication to the Kickstarter model by vetting out potential companies before they are allowed on the site. This site requires prerequisites such as a unit-cost analysis, trademarking, third-party audits, and maintaining funds that were raised in escrow accounts. This allows them to protect investors and force legitimate companies to bring their *A* game.

START-UP FEVER

Next up? CircleUp.com. Circle Up is another up-and-comer focusing on putting startups directly in touch with accredited investors, who then become primary shareholders in the company. You can think of their model as a way to bypass the dozens of pitch meetings with potential angel investors and instead going straight to a large group of angels simultaneously. A very valuable service for those looking to get right down to business, as this is obviously a service geared toward more-seasoned entrepreneurs. Circle Up also prides itself on its major corporate partnerships. These are corporate partners who might just take a shine to one of your spiffy new business models; who knows, maybe they will start you a new division.

Crowdfunder.com is another Kickstarter-type donation-based model, which also integrates a charitable aspect as well—donating different items to charities depending on how much money is raised by the initial public crowdfunding campaign. Sadly, Crowdfunder is another one of the all-or-nothing funding sites; so, if you don't meet your goal, you're kind of screwed. I would use this one with caution for that reason.

AngelList.com is another cutting-edge site built on the backs of Silicon Valley tech-architects. I love AngelList because it also serves as a job board. This site attracts some of the best and the brightest in the tech world. AngelList has been hailed as one of the most innovative concepts by almost all of the relevant industry trade magazines: truly helping to reinvent the tech sector wheel, while speeding up the good idea mechanisms of the business world.

Fundable is another Kickstarter twist that allows users to either donate directly to the company or become a part shareholder with their investment money. The site charges prospective entrepreneurs $99 dollars per month and 3.5% of any funding raised through the site. Again, these models could definitely become the banks for the 22nd century and beyond. As investors start speaking with their dollars, money will talk and bad businesses will walk. Finally, human beings (not consumers) will get to vote with their dollars in the crowdfunding court of public opinion.

Although I would say that the most interesting model to date has come from WeFunder. WeFunder is a crowdfunding site which acts as an intermediary between investors and owners, freeing up time so the owners can focus on building the business instead of attending to 100 micro-investors. This is a valuable site that will allow companies a lot of room to work. In my opinion, this seems like a more sustainable way to acquire legitimate large-scale funding going forward. The good part is: investors will still retain voting rights and stock privileges, unlike most of the other crowdfunding models!

There is surely a crowdfunding site out there to meet your needs no matter what type of business you choose to start. Although many of these sites seem to be running hot to cold very quickly, in the future this market will stabilize—opening up more leeway for social activism and inventiveness. Currently, many crowd-funders are too focused on social media or larger investors. This strategy seems to be holding things back a bit. Yet, sooner or later, everyone will begin to see the bigger picture and crowdfunding will be off to the races. I feel like crowdfunding truly has the potential to change every area of our economic lives and below I have included a list of ideas on what this renaissance may look like.

Possible uses for crowdfunding in the future...

- ✓ Using it as a way to pay people to lose weight. Have companies sponsor people's personal weight loss and give them rebates based upon how much weight they lose by using their products.

- ✓ Using crowdfunding to create innovative recipes from chefs. Hiring them via crowdfunding to divulge their best recipes.

- ✓ Hiring snowboarders to invent new tricks.

- ✓ Commission artistic works on a budget for community centers.

- ✓ Funding for educational video games.

- ✓ We could totally reinvent homeschooling by using the internet to "hire children" to go out and learn about the subjects their teachers were supposed to be teaching, effectively training students to teach themselves. Use the 30,000 per year in tax money to pay ambitious students who want to go and learn things on their own, which will enable smart children to finish school faster—and gain more independent skills in the process.

- ✓ Hire people to research alternative historical viewpoints on subjects of all kinds.

- ✓ Create a voting mechanism to help universities adopt more cutting-edge textbooks.

- ✓ Eliminate the no-bid governmental contracts by offering them publicly.

- ✓ Use crowdfunding to create new production items for 3-D printers so that more people can start producing their own items via this technology.

✓ Creating an online gold-conversion website, allowing users to trade in their crypto-currencies for current market rates.

✓ Creating an online international Forex-type system for startups, where you can invest in different companies around the world.

✓ Have a crowdfunding site on which children choose the ideas that they want to see funded.

✓ Hiring authors to write books on subjects that interest society at-large.

✓ Using crowdfunding to inspire contests for new commercial/personal achievements.

✓ Allow students a platform to get college funding by utilizing an ongoing loan crowdfunding system.

✓ Raise money to reforest the war-torn impoverished communities...www.foresttheworld.com...we could go around and beautify places all around Los Angeles—particularly in poverty-stricken areas. The biggest problem with inner-city ghettos is the fact that they are strictly concrete. Everything within sight is manmade and artificial. If we could introduce plant life back into these urban deserts, these areas might start to thrive again.

✓ Fund social projects to clean up bad parts of town.

✓ Take funding out of politicians hands and put it back into the hands of the people.

✓ Find ways to fund public and community projects.

✓ People could crowd-fund alternative types of community schools for children.

START-UP FEVER

✓ Fund pet adoption rescues via crowdfunding.

Steady will the road be out of technological depravity and into a sustainable future. Obviously, I present these ideas not as an all-inclusive list, but as a starting point to further individuality and balance within the business communities of the future. If we are going to have a beautiful world to live in during the next 100 years, it's only going to be due to a lot of reorientation of current business practices and methods. Although the cases of out-and-out physical murder have gone down in the world, the cases of spiritual suicides of the soul have never been higher. People are dying psychologically younger and younger; and unless we are careful, we really might turn into a pack of post-human iPhone zombies. As any tech café luncheon will tell you: people talk to their technology more than they talk to each other. Philosophically speaking, we have to wonder: if we are communicating in some digital code via the internet, are we actually, truly, communicating? Does the internet represent our subconscious, the omnipresence of a god-type figure, or none of the above? Again, we need to reevaluate technology's role in our lives and determine how far we are prepared to go into the Matrix.

Ch. 9

Mission Equilibrium

For America to regain its former economic luster, we must first start by addressing all of the glaring problems staring us in the face on a day-to-day basis. In just 100 short years, we have managed to all but ruin a country that prided itself on its autonomy and self-reliance. In 2014, almost nobody in our culture is self-sufficient. Some depend on other corporations; others depend on their families; and still others depend on the government. It is very rare to meet an individual who has taken the time to totally free himself from the mass psychosis of the common citizen. The free individuals you do find might not even admit to their pursuit of individualism until you get to know them.

There are some really killer entrepreneurs who have strong family units out there and who help build up their local communities; but, frankly, we need reinforcements. This is an area in which I have found older entrepreneurs to be much better role models. The young kids are still stuck thinking that money will buy them balance and sanity. Recreational activities can be very healthy, but sleeping with a stranger and chugging a fifth of vodka every weekend doesn't do much for your emotional welfare—or your liver! People have become addicted to unrepentantly wasting all of their creative energies via rampant fornication and an obsession with social acclaim. For thousands of years, the ego has ruled mankind with an iron fist. To escape its clutches took determined adepts and a lifetime of dedicated self-discovery. It's high time the business community starts to integrate this quest of self-discovery as well. There has to be a way of conducting business which is not completely ego driven. In time, I know that the solutions will arrive, as humanity is one of the four great powers of the world.

Verse 25, Tao Te Ching

There was something formless and perfect
before the universe was born.
It is serene. Empty.
Solitary. Unchanging.
Infinite. Eternally present.
It is the mother of the universe.
For lack of a better name,
I call it the Tao.t flows through all things,
inside and outside, and returns
to the origin of all things.
The Tao is great.
The universe is great.
Earth is great.
Man is great.
These are the four great powers.
Man follows the earth.
Earth follows the universe.
The universe follows the Tao.

The Tao follows only itself.
(from http://acc6.its.brooklyn.cuny.edu/
~phalsall/texts/taote-v3.html)

Instead of dealing with our emotions in a healthy way, over half of the populace has instead taken to drugs and other forms of self-medication to repress their existential concerns—a trend that could take many years to reverse. America has a drug problem and the central banks have effectively become our drug dealers, giving us just enough juice to keep us addicted. We truly are living in a *Brave New World*-type culture, where numbing out reality is the preferred method of control.

In this day and age, family time constitutes going home and turning on the old slave box, hanging with the kids for a few minutes (if applicable), having some "snuggle time," and passing out. This doesn't exactly leave much time to cultivate a deeper understanding of the cosmos. In ages past, we could rely on the village elder, shaman, sage, or leader to guide us toward these subjects and shed insight on their own arduous quest into selfhood; yet, in modern times, this crucial role has been left relatively vacant. Worse yet, the new form of spiritual leadership has deliberately led many people astray!

Even though we employ more methods of communication than any other period in human history, somehow humanity is losing its basic one-on-one communication ability. Perhaps staring at the screens all day is finally taking its toll on humanity. Who wants to live in a world where we have to stare at a digital screen all day? Oh yeah, most of the kids, that's who! Why is this happening? Is it a learned behavior? Or do these screens represent a kind of false spiritual stimulation to replace what is lacking within the family unit? Anyone who has looked into the subjects of sacred symbolism knows that the subconscious mind responds more to symbols than it does to the spoken word. This is how the advertisers and PR folks have been able to brainwash societies into worshipping false role models—role models who are spiritually demonstrable. On one level, we know that these people are vastly immoral; but on another level, we crave the symbolic meanings behind their subliminal marketing techniques.

Predictive programming has left us in very dangerous territory when it comes to consumer free will. Can we really consider our own thoughts "free thinking" if some advertising super computer somewhere knows what we are going to do before we do? Can we say the machines are smarter than us or are we the ones turning into the machines? This whole hive-mind/*Matrix* scenario is something we really need to think about before we run headlong into a techno utopia, which could quickly reach a point of no return. Do you want to be a robot? I know I don't.

The crazy part is that as advanced as we think our technology may be, it in no way competes with the complex perfection that exists within nature. With all the king's horses and all the king's men, no scientist could ever begin to invent a living organism such as a tree: a task that might seem simple on the surface, but is ultimately far beyond the human intellect—at least in its current state of spiritual atrophy.

Obviously, I must also implicate myself in this diatribe, as I am no anti-technology purist. This book was written on a computer screen, not some handprint, typeset, contraption. I use an iPhone, I am on my laptop a lot, and I like watching enriching movies; so I'm not some form of Amish revolutionary. I merely want to thrust some of the deeper economic questions into the public debate. Our answers probably don't lie in turning away from technology altogether, but instead using technologies with a grave reverence for their destructive potentials. In a country that pops out nuclear missiles like Chiclets, I don't think a little forethought is a bad plan. Technology has served to debase us and drive us further into fantasyland; but with proper care, it can also help us to find ourselves. I know that there are deeply spiritual types of technology out there, many of them stemming from the Nikola Tesla school of thought; but, it's hard to say what level of technology the human species can handle at this juncture. The true question being: how can we use these tools wisely?

The internet has been invaluable to anyone pursuing a spiritual self-awakening, so we can deduce that everything has a good and bad side to it! Obviously, crowdfunding relies upon the internet in its current incarnation, so, again, we are led back to our modernity in the name of balance. However technology plays into our future as a species, creating a technological infrastructure that does not promote ecocide is a good starting point.

It is interesting to note that many of the tribal and more rural agrarian cultures are much happier than us in the western hemisphere. Which begs the question: how much peace of mind has technology really brought us? Hopefully, our future creations will provide a legitimate pathway towards a society that promotes individuality, not just control-based innovation. Again, I think less is more is a philosophy that should always be applied in this realm.

If we are going to be hell bent on making "screens" a long-term implementation within our culture, perhaps people should at least be educated upon the deeper existential underpinnings of what these "screens" really represent. Since all of modern technology has arisen from the human mind, it would make sense that all of these technologies are just an external representation of our innate inner abilities. Even though humanity lacks the spiritual wherewithal to decide our own fate, we can still be a very crafty bunch when we choose to be.

It can be argued that the television is one of the primary drivers of all capitalism. Without television we would not be able to learn about all of the things we are supposed to do in life to attain true fulfillment. Television represents the most powerful psychological alteration device mankind has ever seen. This subject has been covered in many other great works, most notably Neil Postman's "Amusing Ourselves to Death"—as well as Michael Tsarion's subversive use of sacred symbolism lectures. Television has really replaced the dog in the role of "Man's Best Friend." It greets us in the morning, amuses us when we are down, stimulates our sexual drives, and tucks us in to sleep at night—all under the inconspicuous guise of entertainment. To put it bluntly, most people are abject servants of their television and they don't even know it. Obviously, YouTube isn't wholly comprised of enriching content, but at least the escapism-to-enrichment ratio is a bit better in my estimation. Their schedules are determined by its programming and their moods are dictated by its messages. To put it bluntly, television has made many people its bitch!

As of yet, television has not yet entered into the crowdfunding conversation, but I fear the time is not far off. Soon enough, the psychic vultures will attempt to pervert this fiscal medium as well; there might even be a home shopping network for crowdfunding. Who knows what's in store? Rest assured: good always attracts evil, so is the nature of the universe.

Fearless

Aside from a small group of psychologically secure leaders left in the world, we have largely been left to fend for ourselves in an uncertain universe. That being the case, we need to be as prepared as possible when we take up the grand quest of life—a quest that can lead us to true fulfillment or into hundreds of dead ends, depending on our decisions. I don't have to tell you that the world can sometimes be a difficult place. It's easy to get lost among crowds of people who don't know their own spiritual motivations—or worse yet, people who have taken it upon themselves to hide the truth of our reality. If we are ever to make this transition into a prosperous economy successfully, we must not fear letting go of our habituation or our past cultural norms. We must be comfortable moving into a new era in economic existence. I can assure you that there is nothing hip about being a slave. There is nothing hip about having 60% of your money taken away in taxes every month. There is nothing hip about working in a job that forces you to shut down your inner morality or spiritual development. I know this because I have lived in "that world" enough to rebuke it. Anyone who has truly seen the suffering of our world for what it is knows that turning back is not an option. In the words of Lao Tzu: "If I give up who I am, I become who I might be." We must all begin to let go of who we think we are so that we may become something greater.

With my set of optimistic eyes, I know that this new wave of emotionally centered, subconsciously aware, young entrepreneurs represents an opportunity to get things back on the right track. Cultivation of meaningful spiritual progress is a constant battle in this dimension. As a new generation of young people blossom, we must understand our duty to stand up and protect the sacred things in this world. The first and foremost of these sacred creations are the children. Children are not able to speak freely about their views on structural reforms in the adult world, so we must speak for them. So, if you don't feel like cleaning up your karma for your own sake, do it for the kids. They will thank you for it someday!

I hope this book has persuaded you to walk with me outside of the boundaries demarcated by comfort and convenience and, instead, take a journey with me into the uncharted realms of predictive economic reconstruction. As strange as it may seem, the biggest problem most of us will ever face is staring right at us every time we look in the mirror. I keep looking and that same guy keeps looking back at me; in fact, I'm beginning to think he's following me! But in all seriousness, it's about time we start getting to know this strange critter looking back at us in the mirror—and figuring out who and why this strange person keeps getting out of bed, going to work, if just to meet an uncertain fate? You have arrived in the universe, at this exact time, at this exact place; now, we just need to figure out what for. Some people live their whole lives without really talking to their inner self in an attempt to get to know the *who*, *what*, and *why* of their existence.

Until we are able to understand the meaning behind that person we call our reflection, we will have a heck of a time finding meaning out in the land of lost souls known as Earth. All uncertainty aside, you can rest assured that until the day you die that little critter in the mirror will be subtly asking you to decode the purpose of your presence. Why have you come and where will you need to go to make your life meaningful? Whether your best friend or your mortal foe: that little person looking back at you in the mirror will end up deciding your fate.

Once and a while, out in the "real" world, you stumble across problems so large, so multifaceted, so complex, they can only be referred to it as enigmatic. American economics presents us with just such a series of enigmatic problems: problems so complex they could only emanate from within the human soul. Only humanity's endless sense of curiosity, love for hierarchy, and gluttonous appetite for catharsis could have created such a complex economic world. The current world banking system truly represents a Gordian knot for the ages. Being that the depths of the human super-consciousness has created such a complex system of making a living, it would make sense that the answers to just such problems would also emanate from within. So, just in the nick of time, here comes a series of grassroots solutions known as crowdfunding. An economic vehicle created by entrepreneurs, for entrepreneurs, and with the dynamic human spirit in mind!

To all of your innovators and entrepreneurial types out there, I say good luck and I wish you all the best in your travels and endeavors in this wild world we call Earth! For further inquiries, please feel free to email me at Startupfever9@gmail.com. Or check out my websites at www.crowdfundforlife.com and www.astrologybyaustin.com. Again, I thank you so much for your time and I look forward to a bigger and brighter economic future through crowdfunding!

Acknowledgements

This book is dedicated to my mother, my father, Dr. Wu, Michael, and Michael Tsarion.

To my mom for being my inspiration for perseverance, and for showing me what perpetual optimism in business looks like. I also wanted to give her big thanks for not killing me in my teenage years. To my Dad for teaching me the value of hard work, and determination, and the fact that with true leadership anything is possible. To Michael for helping open the door to this higher phase of my spiritual life, and for all of the perpetual knowledge you have bestowed upon me. To Dr. Wu for helping me in more ways than I can acutely describe, and for teaching me how to help myself. And last but not least to Michael Tsarion for teaching me most of what I know about selfhood, philosophy, divination, and the true purpose of life.

More information

You will find more information on crowdfunding at
www.crowdfundforlife.com

Or contact Austin via email:
Startupfever9@gmail.com